小學生 Grammar

圖解教程和練習

句子文法

配合香港教育局建議學習目標編寫
小學二至五年級適用

編著 李雪熒

- 21篇圖解趣味句式教程
- 覆蓋小學重點文法學習目標
- 70組不同程度練習（附答案）
- 讓各級學生輕鬆學好 Grammar

序言

各位小朋友：

在香港讀書，你們無可避免要學好英文。無論你喜歡學英文，還是一見到雞腸般的英文句子就想找個洞去躲避，英文仍然無時無刻存在於你的學習和生活環境之中。總之，你是躲也躲不了的。既然是這樣，最好的方法，就是直接面對它。

你們或許會發現，有些同學英文學得很輕鬆，有些卻學得很辛苦，某同學的英文考試成績總是非常優異，而自己和另一些同學卻普普通通。為甚麼會這樣呢？是不是那些學得較好的同學較聰明呢？當然不是！其實，只要大家學英文時，懂得靈活運用，融會貫通，平時多留意身邊事物，如零食包裝上的英文、地鐵車廂裡或廣告上標示的英文，再結合老師在課堂上教的文法知識，你就會覺得學英文是一件輕鬆愉快的事情。

為了幫助大家學好英文，本書在教授各種文法時，不但為你詳細剖析句子的文法結構，而且還提供大量例句，鞏固你的文法知識。大家掌握了文法知識後，不妨到「文法加油站」做一些練習；你還可以到「挑戰站」挑戰難度較高的題目，一試身手。

有了這本書，學英文Grammar，從此變得很輕鬆！

李雪熒

作者簡介

李雪熒，香港中文大學社會科學榮譽學士及北京師範大學文學碩士，深信學習是一場愉快的遊戲，曾任創意寫作班、繪畫班、校本學習支援導師，著有《學生專題研習天書》、《我的第一本經典英文100童詩》、《小學生學理財經濟55通識課》、《彈升孩子學習戰鬥力》、《潛移默化的睡前德育小故事——100教訓》、《中國謀略故事》、《親子枕邊100成語故事III》、《高效孩子的12個習慣》、《戒掉孩子壞習慣》、《態度決定孩子一生》、《生活細節教出大道理》等。

目錄
Table of Contents

小學生學 *Grammar* ——句子文法

完整句子
Complete Sentence

東東正在聽音樂，小花不會做算術題，想問東東。她說：「Please come here.」（請你過來一下。）可是，東東沒有聽見，於是小花再說一遍：「Can you come here?」（你過來這兒，可以嗎？）東東仍沒有聽見。小花生氣了，他走到東東面前大叫說：「You are deaf!」（你是聾的！）東東覺得有點莫名其妙。

大家有沒有留意到，小花所說的三句話都是完整句子（Complete sentence）。甚麼是完整句子呢？完整句子就是**可以表達完整意思的句子，通常句子包括主詞（Subjects）和動詞（Verbs），有些句子還會加上其他字詞**，如形容詞、副詞等來幫助說明意思。例如：

Sam runs.
山姆跑步。

Alan and David played computer game.
阿倫和大衛玩電腦遊戲。

「Sam runs.」由主詞和動詞組成，是意思完整的句子。「Alan and David played computer game.」也是完整句子，它由主詞、動詞和其他字詞組成，能表達完整的意思。其他例子有：

Judy cried.
茱迪哭。

The baby laughs.
那嬰兒笑。

Mandy and Simon will get married next week.
下星期蔓迪和西門將會結婚。

I like ice cream.
我喜歡冰淇淋。

陳述句

完整句子可分為陳述句（Statement）、問句（Question）和感嘆句（Exclamation）。**陳述句用來描寫人物和事物**，通常以標點符號「.」作結，如「I like swimming.」（我喜歡游泳。）、「I go to school.」（我上學。）等等。大家看看這個句子：

Daddy likes coffee.
爸爸喜歡咖啡。

「Daddy likes coffee.」由主詞、動詞、其他字詞和「.」組成，是意思完整的陳述句。其他例子有：

Miss Lee teaches English.
李老師教英文。

Tom will go to India next week.
下星期湯姆將會去印度。

Mommy is cooking.
媽媽在做飯。

問句

問句是用來詢問有關的人和事物，通常以標點符號「?」作結，如「Can I see you?」（我可以見你嗎？）、「What is it?」（這是甚麼？）等等，大家看看這個句子：

Can you come here?
你可以過來這兒嗎？

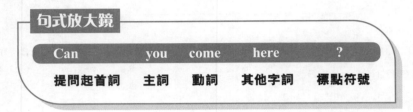

句式放大鏡

Can	you	come	here	?
提問起首詞	主詞	動詞	其他字詞	標點符號

「Can you come here?」由提問起首詞、主詞、動詞、其他字詞和「?」組成意思完整的問句。其他例子有：

What is your name?
你的名字是甚麼？

Is it your dog?
牠是你的狗嗎？

Will you come tomorrow?
明天你會來嗎？

感嘆句

感嘆句是用來表達強烈的情緒或感受，通常以標點符號「!」作結，如「What a lovely girl!」（可愛的女孩！）、「The dog is loudy!」（那隻狗很吵！）等等，大家看看這個句子：

The dress is beautiful!
那裙子很漂亮！

句式放大鏡

The dress	is	beautiful	!
主詞	動詞	其他字詞	標點符號

「The dress is beautiful!」由主詞、動詞、其他字詞和「!」組成，是意思完整的感嘆句。感嘆句有數種表達式，包括「How＋形容詞」，如「How big!」（很大！）；或只使用形容詞，如「Great!」（棒！）。其他例子有：

What a big house!　很大的房子！　　How fast!　　真快！
Good!　　　　　　好！　　　　　You are foolish!　你是個笨蛋

文法加油站

練習一

請在完整句子的空格內加 ☑ ，不是完整句子的加 ☒ 。

1. Wilson is playing football. ☐
2. How big! ☐
3. The puppy is cute! ☐
4. Can you call me tonight? ☐
5. Have you been to Hong Kong? ☐
6. I will visit. ☐
7. In the house. ☐
8. I live in Hong Kong Island. ☐
9. I do not like doing homework. ☐
10. Sun. ☐

練習二

請判斷下列句子。

陳述句（S） 問句（Q） 感嘆句（E）

1. David laughs. _____
2. Joey is playing piano. _____
3. What a hardworking girl! _____
4. Can Alison sing? _____
5. He will leave Hong Kong tomorrow. _____
6. She feels very happy. _____
7. How fast! _____
8. Will you go tomorrow? _____
9. Kitty did it very well. _____
10. A great work! _____

挑戰站

試重組下列句子。

1. my / Bobby / dog / . / is

_____

2. were / Carrie and Janice / last year / . / in the same class

_____

3. Have / come / ? / he

_____

4. handsome / A / ! / boy

_____

5. ! / How / beautiful

_____

6. go hiking / with Sidney / . / I

_____

7. Have / you / read / ? / this book

_____

8. watched / . / at ten o'clock / Daddy / football match

_____

9. cried / . / She

_____

10. had / in Shek O / We / a barbecue / . / last week

_____

祈使句：
必要和緊急的事
Imperatives: Positive and Negative Form

小樂站在馬路前，交通燈轉了紅色，他見馬路上沒有車，打算衝紅燈，一個老婆婆大叫說：「Don't cross the road. It's red light.」（不要過馬路！現在是紅燈。）小樂沒有理會老婆婆的警告，在紅燈時過馬路，老婆婆再大叫說：「Look out! A car is coming.」（注意！一架車快來了。）只見一輛車急促前進，小樂剛好站在馬路中間，眼見那輛車快要碰上自己，小樂竟然怕得走不動。幸好，這時交通燈轉了綠燈。

小樂不遵守交通規則實在不對，而老婆婆對小樂所說的話都屬於祈使句（Imperatives）。祈使句是英語中其中一種句子結構，主要用來**發出警告、命令、指令和指示，以及提出建議或請求。**

祈使句的肯定句

祈使句可分為肯定句（Positive Form）和否定句（Negative Form）。祈使句的肯定句形式是**以動詞基本形作起首詞**，一般沒有主詞（Subject），如「Look out!」（注意！）、「Be careful!」（小心！）等等。大家看看這個句子：

Be careful. The water is hot.
小心！那些水是熱的。

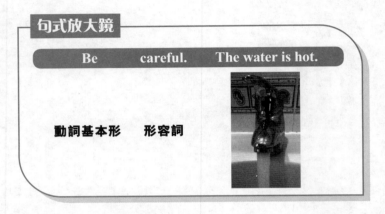

句式放大鏡

Be　　　careful.　　The water is hot.

動詞基本形　　形容詞

「Be careful. The water is hot.」是祈使句的肯定句形式（Positive Form），大家留意「Be careful.」一句中的「Be」是動詞基本形。這個句子用來向人發出警告。其他例子有：

Look out! The bus is coming.
注意！那輛巴士正駛來。

Be polite to the teacher.
對老師要有禮貌。

Stop smoking or you'll be sick.
停止吸煙，吸煙會令你生病的。

除了發出警告和命令外，大家還可以使用祈使句的肯定句形式來提出建議和請求。這種祈使句的形式是以「Let's」（即「Let us」）作起首詞，然後接動詞基本形，如「Let's go!」（我們走吧！）等等。大家看看以下句子：

Let's dance.
我們跳舞吧。

句式放大鏡

Let's　　　dance.
起首詞　　動詞基本形

「Let's dance.」是祈使句的肯定句形式（Positive Form），由「Let's起首詞＋動詞基本形」組成，用來向人提出建議。其他例子有：

Let's stop here.
我們在這兒結束吧。

Let's go to the museum.
我們去博物館吧。

祈使句的否定句

祈使句的否定句形式通常在動詞基本形前面加「Don't」（不要），表示命令不要做的意思。大家看看這個句子：

Don't run in the corridor.
不要在走廊跑.

句式放大鏡

Don't	run	in the corridor.
起首詞	動詞基本形	

「Don't run in the corridor.」是祈使句的否定句形式（Negative Form），由「Don't起首詞＋動詞基本形」組成，用來向人發出命令。其他例子有：

Don't talk in the library.
不要在圖書館談話。

Don't smoke in public place.
不要在公共場所吸煙。

> ！ 祈使句可給人建議，如果提供建議的人是「我」，可以用「Let」＋「me」＋動詞基本形，例如：「Let me try again.」（讓我再試一次。）、「Let me contact Mrs. Fong.」（讓我聯絡方太太吧。）。

2

文法加油站

練習一

下列句子哪些是祈使句？請在祈使句的方格上加 ☑，不是祈使句的加 ☒。

1. Kenny and Ken are good friends. ☐

2. Don't talk in the library. ☐

3. Let me show you how. ☐

4. Don't watch TV after 10:00PM. ☐

5. Miranda has two brothers. ☐

6. I don't like Maths. ☐

7. Look out! The bus is coming. ☐

8. Be careful. The floor is wet. ☐

9. Don't be rudely. Be polite to your parent. ☐

10. Write your name and address here. ☐

練習二

請將正確的答案寫在橫線上。

1. The baby is cute. _____ me play with her.

2. _____ play computer game after 8:00PM.

3. _____ careful. There are some glasses on the floor.

4. _____ feed the dog with fish.

5. _____ eating or you'll be fat.

6. _____ honest. _____ the policeman the truth.

7. _____ up now or you'll be late.

8. _____ go to the beach this weekend.

9. _____ your name on the examination paper.

10. _____ jump on the see-saw. It's dangerous.

挑戰站

請參看例子，圈出下列祈使句中的錯誤，並將正確的答案寫在右邊的橫線上。

例子：

Don't (watched) TV when you are doing homework.   watch

1. Kept quiet! Grandma is sleeping.   _____

2. Doesn't cross the road. The traffic light is red.   _____

3. Don't is rudely.   _____

4. Been honest to your friends.   _____

5. Looking out! The bus is coming.   _____

6. Let visit Aunt Amy this Sunday.   _____

7. Let me talked to you later.   _____

8. Woke up or you'll miss the school bus.   _____

9. Listening! The bird is singing.   _____

10. Don't running. It's slippery.   _____

簡單現在式：肯定句

Simple Present Tense: Positive Form

　　樂樂早上起來，一面拉開窗簾一面說：「The weather is fine today.」（今天天氣很好）。吃早餐前，他先跟爸爸和媽媽說：「Good morning, daddy and mummy. I love you.」（爸爸、媽媽早晨！我愛你們。）再對妹妹說：「We wash our hands before having breakfast.」（我們吃早餐前先洗手。）吃過早餐後，他看看手錶，對妹妹說：「I think you have to hurry up. The school bus leaves at seven o'clock.」（我想你要快點了。校車在七時離開。）

　　樂樂一個早上所說的話，都運用了現在式時態中的肯定句形式。現在式時態中的肯定句形式主要用來表達現在的情況或狀態，即**現在做的事情，也用來表達習慣、事實、現在真確的事情、現時的想法、計劃和時間表**。你們能說出樂樂所說的話，屬於哪一種嗎？

The weather is fine today.　　　　　　⇨　現時真確的事情
I love you.　　　　　　　　　　　　　⇨　事實
We wash our hands before having breakfast.　⇨　習慣
I think you have to hurry up.　　　　　⇨　現時的想法
The school bus leaves at seven o'clock.　⇨　時間表

大家看看以下的時間線圖：

Past　　　　　　　Present　　　　　　Future
過去　　　　　　　現在　　　　　　　將來

問：What do Peter and Joe do everyday?
　　彼得和祖每天在做甚麼？

答：Peter and Joe play computer game everyday.
　　彼得和祖每天在玩電腦遊戲。

句式放大鏡

Peter and Joe	play	computer game	everyday.
	動詞基本形		表示現在的時間的字詞

「Peter and Joe play computer game everyday.」是現在式的肯定句形式（The Positive Form），大家留意句子裡的動詞「play」是動詞基本形。在表示現在的動作、行為、計畫或想法時，必須使用動詞基本形。另外，當主詞是「I」（即第一身單數）、「We」（即第一身複數）、「You」（即第二身單數和複數）、「They」（第三身複數），表達現在的動作或行為時，必須使用動詞基本形，如上面的句子中，主詞是「Peter and Joe」兩個人，等同第三身複數的「They」，因此，句中的動詞就要使用基本形；而當主詞是第三身單數（即He、She、It）時，必須在動詞基本形的尾部加「s」或者「es」。

例如：Mandy plays tennis with her friend.
　　　曼迪和朋友打網球。

　　　Benjamin goes to school by bus.
　　　本傑明坐巴士上學。

甚麼時候用現在式？

一般來説，描述現在發生的事情、行為、想法時，句中通常都有一些表示頻率的時間字詞，如today（今天）、everyday（每天）、often（有時）、sometimes（有時）、always（經常/常常/時時）、usually（通常）等等。所以，當我們在句中看到這些字詞時，就知道這個句子所表達的時態是現在式。

例如：
1. He often eats sushi.
他有時吃壽司。

2. I go to swim everyday .
我每天去游泳。

3. Mummy always sweeps the floor.
媽媽常常掃地。

4. Daddy usually goes to office by MTR.
爸爸有時乘坐地下鐵路上班。

> 在現在式的句子中，動詞「be」是「am、is、are」的基本形。大家做練習時，如果題目只給你「be」作提示，到底要使用「am、is、are」中的哪一個呢？其實方法很簡單，只需看看句中的主詞，就可以知道答案了。例如主詞是「I」，則動詞應使用「am」；主詞是「He、She、It」，則動詞應使用「is」，主詞是「You、They、We」，則動詞應使用「are」。

文法加油站

練習一

請參看例子，在現在式的句子加 ☑，並把句中現在式的動詞圈出來，不是現在式的句子則加 ☒。

例子：She likes painting. ☑

1. Dickson and Ken are in the same class.
2. Kathy always goes to school on foot.
3. I went to library last Sunday.
4. You like playing football.
5. We had one brother.
6. They are my grandparents.
7. He is a teacher.
8. She wants some sandwiches.
9. The weather is not good.
10. The train leaves at ten o'clock.

簡單現在式：肯定句 Simple Present Tense : Positive Form

請將正確的答案寫在橫線上。

1. The baby _____ (be) cute.

2. She _____ (have) two sisters.

3. I _____ (be) eleven years old.

4. Cats _____ (like) fish.

5. He _____ (swim) every evening after school.

6. Joey and Kelly _____ (be) good friends.

7. Kenny always _____ (wake) up at seven o'clock.

8. It _____ (be) sunny today.

9. You sometimes _____ (watch) football match at night.

10. They _____ (want) some fruit juice.

挑戰站

請參看例子，找出下列句子中的錯誤，並將正確的答案寫在右邊的橫線上。

例子：

| My Aunt always (watched) TV every night. | watches |

1. My sister were ten years old today. _____

2. My name was Penny Lee. _____

3. Miss Chan come from America. _____

4. We goes hiking this coming Sunday. _____

5. He playes football every day. _____

6. I sometimes visited my grandparents on Saturday. _____

7. Gladys and Amy likes dancing. _____

8. You usually went to school by bus. _____

9. The train leave at 2:30PM every day. _____

10. Tammy be a nurse. _____

chapter 4

簡單現在式：否定句

Simple Present Tense: Negative Form

今天是星期天，樂樂不用上學，以下是樂樂早上所說的話。樂樂起床後，說：「do not wake up at six o' clock today.」（今天我不用六時起床。）然後拉開窗簾，說：「The weather is not good.」（天氣不好。）

吃早餐時，他對妹妹說：「We do not hurry up for school bus.（我們不用匆匆忙忙趕校巴。）We do not go to school today.（我們今天不用上學。）」

樂樂星期天早上所說的話，是運用了現在式時態中的否定形式。現在式時態中的**否定形式主要用來否定現在的情況或狀態。**

大家看看以下的時間線圖：

Past　　　　　　Present　　　　　　Future
過去　　　　　　現在　　　　　　將來

問：Do Alan and Sam play computer game?
　　亞倫和森姆玩電腦遊戲嗎？

答：Alan and Sam do not play computer game.
　　亞倫和森姆不是玩電腦遊戲。

問：Are you Sam?
　　你是森姆嗎？

答：I am not Sam.
　　我不是森姆。

句式放大鏡

Alan and Sam	do	not	play	computer game.
	助動詞	否定	動詞基本形	

I	am	not	Sam.
	動詞	否定	

「Alan and Sam do not play computer game.」和「I am not Sam.」都是現在式的否定句形式（The Negative Form）。

do not 和 is not

大家留意「Alan and Sam do not play computer game.」一句裡的動詞基本形「play」前面有「do not」。這是助動詞（「do」）加否定形式（「not」），表示否定在現在的時態裡所描述的事情。而「I am not Sam.」一句裡的動詞「am」後面接「not」，也是具有否定在現在的時態裡所描述某事情的意思。

試觀察及比較以下各項：

主詞	「Be」動詞		一般動詞	
	肯定句	否定句	肯定句	否定句
「I」	am	am not	like	do not like
「He、She、It」	is	is not	likes	does not like
「You、We、They」	are	are not	like	do not like

從上表可以知道，當主詞是「I」時，如果動詞是「am」，它的否定形式就是「am＋not」；如果動詞是一般動詞，如「like」、「go」、「want」等，它的否定形式就是「do＋not＋動詞基本形」。

當主詞是「He、She、It」時，如果動詞是「is」，它的否定形式就是「is＋not」；如果動詞是一般動詞，如「like」、「go」、「want」等，它的否定形式就是「does＋not＋動詞基本形」。

當主詞是「You、We、They」時，如果動詞是「are」，它的否定形式就是「are＋not」；如果動詞是一般動詞，如「like」、「go」、「want」等，它的否定形式就是「do＋not＋動詞基本形」。

例如： I am not Tom.　　　　　　　　He is not Sam.
　　　 我不是湯姆。　　　　　　　　他不是森姆。

　　　 I do not want coffee.　　　　　He does not go to school.
　　　 我不要咖啡。　　　　　　　　他不是上學去。

　　　 They are not in the same class.　They do not like this game.
　　　 他們不是同一班。　　　　　　他們不喜歡這個遊戲。

> ! 　「am not」、「is not」、「are not」的縮寫分別是「ain't」、「isn't」、「aren't」。而「do not」和「does not」的縮寫分別是「don't」和「doesn't」。

文法加油站

練習一

請參看例子，在現在式的否定形式句子加 ☑，並把句中的否定式圈出來，不是的則加 ☒。

例子：

She likes cooking.	☒
He does not go to library.	☑

1. Danny and Kenny are good friends.

2. Daddy does not go to office.

3. I am not ten years old.

4. You do not like playing badminton.

5. We do not have three toy cars.

6. She is not my grandma.

7. He is a lawyer.

8. She does not want some rice.

9. The weather is fine.

10. The plane does not arrive at four o'clock.

請將正確的答案寫在橫線上。

1. The dog _____ (be not) big.

2. Mrs. Wong _____ (not have) three children.

3. He _____ (be not) my cousin.

4. Kitten _____ (not sleep) under the table.

5. Gordon _____ (not want) chocolate cake.

6. Amy and Jason _____ (be not) brother and sister.

7. Ray _____ (not go) home at twelve o'clock.

8. It _____ (be not) rainy day.

9. I _____ (be not) a boy.

10. They _____ (not watch) TV at night.

挑戰站

請參看例子，檢查下列句子中的否定式是否錯誤，並將正確的句子寫下來。

例子：Ruby is not watched TV at night.

<u>Ruby does not watch TV at night.</u>

1. Chris do not likes coffee.

_____

2. I is not a teacher.

_____

3. Mr. Smith are not come from Australia.

_____

4. We do not goes to the beach this weekend.

_____

5. I am not playes tennis with Sue.

_____

6. Miranda and Kitty does not visited Lily this Saturday.

_____

7. Greg and Amy does not likes singing.

_____

8. Mummy do not go to supermarket.

_____

9. The dog am not small.

_____

10. Charlie are not my classmate.

_____

chapter 5

簡單現在式：問句

Simple Present Tense: Question Form

　　樂樂的妹妹總愛問個不停，以下是妹妹常常問的問題。妹妹在公園看見小鳥和小狗，就會問：「Does grandpa like birds?」（爺爺喜歡小鳥嗎？），「Do you like dogs?」（你喜歡狗嗎？）在學校裡，見到哥哥和他的同學，她會問：「Are they your friends?」（他們是你的朋友嗎？）見到女同學和哥哥打招呼，她總會問：「Is she your classmate?」（她是你的同學嗎？）

　　樂樂覺得在妹妹提問的問題之中，最難回答的問題是：「Am I beautiful?」

　　弟妹愛問個不休，做哥哥或姐姐的有時真的覺得好煩。樂樂的妹妹所說的話，都運用了現在式時態中的問句形式。現在式時態中的問句形式主要用來**提問、查詢現在的情況或狀態，以及現在做的事情。**

大家看看以下的時間線圖：

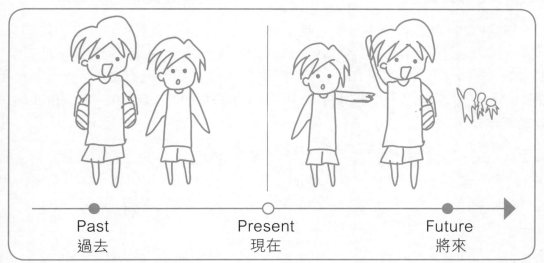

Past
過去

Present
現在

Future
將來

John：Do you like basketball?
約翰說：「你喜歡籃球嗎？」

Simon：Is he your friend?
西門說：「他是你的朋友嗎？」

句式放大鏡

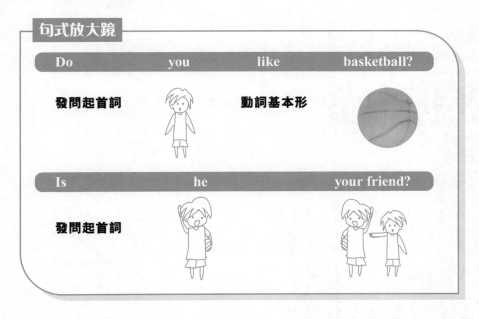

Do	you	like	basketball?
發問起首詞		動詞基本形	

Is	he	your friend?
發問起首詞		

「Do you like basketball?」和「Is he your friend?」是現在式的問句形式（The Question Form），前一句是以助動詞為發問起首詞，後一句是以「be」動詞為發問起首詞。大家留意這兩句的發問起首詞：「Do」和「Is」，這是現在式問句中其中兩種發問的形式，即以助動詞「Do」、「Does」，以及以「be」動詞的現在式「Am」、「Is」、「Are」作發問起首詞。

選擇發問起首詞

那麼，到底甚麼時候用「Do」或「Does」作發問起首詞呢？當主詞是「I」、「We」、「You」、「They」、「Peter and Joe」時，應使用「Do」作發問起首詞；當主詞是「He」、「She」、「It」（第三身單數）時，就要使用「Does」作發問起首詞。另外，大家要記住，當使用「Do」和「Does」作發問起首詞時，主詞後面要接動詞基本形。

以「be」動詞作發問起首詞，甚麼時候用「Am」、「Is」、「Are」呢？當主詞是「I」時，發問起首詞必須是「Am」；當主詞是「You」、「We」、「They」、「Mary and Lily」時，發問起首詞必須是「Are」；當主詞是「He」、「She」、「It」、「Tony」時，發問起首詞必須是「Is」。

例如：

Do Mandy and Kathy like swimming?
曼迪和凱西喜歡游泳嗎？

Does she go to Ocean Park?
她去海洋公園嗎？

Am I beautiful?
我漂亮嗎？

Is Tom a bus driver?
湯姆是巴士司機嗎？

Are they American?
他們是美國人嗎？

文法加油站

練習一

請將正確的答案圈出來。

例子：(Does) / Do she like drawing?

1. Do / Does Dicky and Peggy do homework now?

2. Do / Does you like table tennis?

3. Do / Does we go to Kowloon Bay?

4. Do / Does she want some coffee?

5. Do / Does Summy like ice cream?

6. Do / Does mummy go to supermarket?

7. Do / Does Sam and Sean go to school by school bus?

8. Do / Does Mr. Lee live in Hong Kong Island?

9. Do / Does I give the book to you?

練習二

請將正確的答案圈出來。

例子：Am / Is / (Are) you Mr. Wong?

1. Am / Is / Are I smart boy?

2. Am / Is / Are Jane your sister?

3. Am / Is / Are I hardworking girl?

4. Am / Is / Are it the Great Wall?

5. Am / Is / Are Kitty and Peggy Chinese?

6. Am / Is / Are they your classmates?

7. Am / Is / Are he a fireman?

8. Am / Is / Are she beautiful?

9. Am / Is / Are the weather good?

10. Am / Is / Are your mummy a dancer?

挑戰站

請參看例子，找出下列句子中的錯誤，並將正確的答案寫在右邊的橫線上。

例子：

Does Aunt Judy always (watched) TV at night?	watch
(Does) Jade and Amy go to Tai Po?	Do
(Am) they Japanese?	Are

1. Am Mickey eleven years old? _____

2. Do Penny go to see a movie with Kitty? _____

3. Does Anthony has sisters? _____

4. Do we goes to the beach this Sunday? _____

5. Are he a singer? _____

6. Does I borrow this book from you? _____

7. Am Gladys and Connie good friends? _____

8. Is you Mr. Kennedy? _____

9. Does the train leaves at 6:30PM? _____

10. Are Winnie a bus driver? _____

現在進行式：
肯定句

Present Continuous Tense:
Positive Form

美兒獨個坐在地上哭，嬸嬸問她發生甚麼事了，美兒哭着說：「沒有人跟我玩……」「Frankie is doing homework.」（范克正在做功課。）「Peggy and Rita are helping their mother.」（佩吉和麗塔正在給媽媽幫忙。）「Alan is drawing.」（阿倫正在畫畫。）「Eamon and Sally are playing computer game.」（埃蒙和莎莉正在玩電腦遊戲。）「連我最要好的朋友莎倫也說：'I am reading.'」（我正在看書。）

美兒向嬸嬸描述朋友們正在做甚麼的句子，運用了現在進行式時態中的肯定句形式。現在進行式時態中的肯定句形式主要用來描述**說話時正在進行的動作**。

大家看看以下的時間線圖：

問：What is Joe doing?
　　阿祖正在做甚麼？

答：Joe is running.
　　阿祖正在跑步。

句式放大鏡

Joe	is	running.
	動詞	動詞＋ing

進行式的語法

　　「Joe is running.」是現在進行式的肯定句形式（The Positive Form），大家留意句子裡的動詞必須是「am」、「is」、「are」中其中一個，而描述有關動作的動詞必須在尾部加「ing」，例如「eating」、「drinking」、「watching」等等。

　　大家是否記得甚麼時候使用「am」、「is」、「are」呢？當主詞是「I」時，動詞必須使用「am」；當主詞是「We」、「You」、「They」時，動詞必須使用「are」；當主詞是「He」、「She」、「It」時，動詞就要使用「is」。

例如：I am playing computer game.
　　　我在玩電腦遊戲。

　　　He is watching TV.
　　　他在看電視。

　　　Bill is playing piano.
　　　比爾在彈琴。

They are having a barbecue.
他們在燒烤。

Daddy and mummy are talking with Miss Lee.
爸爸和媽媽正在跟李老師説話。

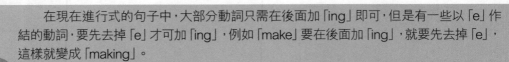

現在進行式：肯定句 Present Continuous Tense : Positive Form

在現在進行式的句子中，大部分動詞只需在後面加「ing」即可，但是有一些以「e」作結的動詞，要先去掉「e」才可加「ing」，例如「make」要在後面加「ing」，就要先去掉「e」，這樣就變成「making」。

另外，英語中有些以輔音字母作結的動詞，如最後的字母前是單一個母音字母，就要重複最後的字母，然後才加「ing」，例如「sit」，加「ing」的話，應該是「sitting」；再如「put」，加「ing」的話，應該是「putting」；「get」加「ing」的話，應該是「getting」。

文法加油站

練習一

請參看例子，把句子寫成現在進行式的肯定句形式。

例子：She drinks.
　　　She is drinking.

1. Kenny and Mandy run away.

　　_____

2. Mummy cooks in the kitchen.

　　_____

3. I take the bus.

　　_____

4. You play football with your classmates.

　　_____

5. We have barbecue.

　　_____

6. They watch TV.

　　_____

7. The bus comes.

　　_____

8. She eats some cookies.

　　_____

9. A dog runs after a cat.

　　_____

10. Adrian puts the book on the table.

　　_____

練習二

請參看例子，將正確的答案寫在橫線上。

例子： make _____make making_____

1. swim _____   9. write _____

2. watch _____   10. read _____

3. get _____   11. sing _____

4. sit _____   12. cook _____

5. run _____   13. fly _____

6. drive _____   14. walk _____

7. have _____   15. cut _____

8. teach _____

挑戰站

請參看例子，找出下列現在進行式的句子中的錯誤，並將正確的答案寫在右邊的橫線上。

例子：

Miss Chan (are) teaching English. _____is_____

My grandpa is (waterring) flowers. _____watering_____

1. My brother is geting fatter. _____

2. Paul and David are makeing model. _____

3. Mr. Cheung am writing in the room. _____

4. We is playing computer game. _____

5. Tom am drawing. _____

6. I am driveing a red racing car. _____

7. Amy and Ruby are cookking in the kitchen. _____

8. You are puting the cup on the table. _____

9. Look! The bus is comeing! _____

10. Daddy is singging. _____

現在進行式：否定句

Present Continuous Tense: Negative Form

桐桐和弟弟東尼躲在房間裡數小時，媽媽覺得奇怪，於是在門外問他們在做甚麼，兩姐弟故作神秘地回答媽媽。桐桐説：「I am not reading. Tony is not reading He is not doing homework.」，東尼説：「I am not doing homework. June is no doing homework. She is not reading.」

兩姐弟在房間裡小聲地笑，原來他們正在給媽媽製作生日禮物。

桐桐和東尼兩姐弟對媽媽所説的話採用了甚麼時態呢？它們又屬於哪一種句子形式？其實，他們所説的是現在進行式時態中的否定句形式。當我們想描述説話時不在進行中的動作時，可以使用現在進行式時態中的否定句形式。

大家看看以下的時間線圖：

Past	Present	Future
過去	現在	將來

問：Is Judy writing?
　　茱迪在寫作嗎？

答：No, Judy is not writing .
　　不，茱迪不是在寫作。

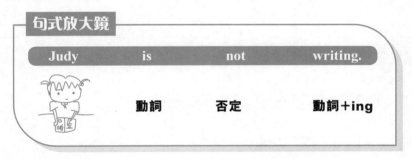

句式放大鏡

Judy	is	not	writing.
	動詞	否定	動詞＋ing

否定句在動詞後接not

「Judy is not writing.」是現在進行式的否定句形式（The Negative Form），它跟肯定句形式一樣，句中的動詞必須是「am」、「is」、「are」中其中一個。而表示否定所描述的動作，就要在動詞後接「not」，變成「am＋not」、「is＋not」和「are＋not」，而描述有關動作的動詞必須在尾部加「ing」，例如「writing」、「reading」、「doing」等等。

例如：I am not doing homework.
　　　我不是在做功課。

He is not reading .
他不是在閱讀。

Alan is not running .
阿倫不是在跑步。

They are not walking .
他們不是在散步。

Stella and Mandy are not washing dishes.
斯特拉和曼迪不是在洗碗。

再次提一提大家要注意以下事情：

在現在進行式的句子中，大部分動詞只需在後面加「ing」即可，但是有一些以「e」作結的動詞，要先去掉「e」才可加「ing」，例如「have」要在後面加「ing」，就要先去掉「e」，這樣就變成「having」。

英語中有些以輔音字母作結的動詞，如最後的字母前是單一個母音字母，就要重複最後的字母，然後才加「ing」，例如「stop」，加「ing」的話，應該是「stopping」。

文法加油站

練習一

請參看例子，利用提供的字詞，寫出現在進行式的否定句形式的句子。

例子：June / walk / in the park / is / not / .

June is not walking in the park.

1. Jessica and May / cook in the kitchen / are / not / .

_____

2. Grandma / sit / on the sofa / is / not / .

_____

3. I / watch / TV / am / not / .

_____

4. You / play / table tennis with Tammy / are / not / .

_____

5. We / make / car model / are / not / .

_____

6. They / wash / dishes / are / not / .

_____

7. The dog / eat / fish / is / not / .

_____

8. Betty / make / sandwiches / is / not / .

_____

9. are / not / Ben and Eric / sing / in the music room / .

_____

10. Janice / put / is / not / the bag on the table / .

_____

請在正確的句子上加 ☑，錯誤的句子上加 ☒。

1. The birds are not singing. ☐

2. Penny and Dennis is not playying badminton. ☐

3. Mr. Wong is not getting stronger. ☐

4. We are not playing chess. ☐

5. Tommy is not reading in the sitting room. ☐

6. I am not talking with May. ☐

7. Cathy and Kitty am not cookking in the kitchen. ☐

8. You are not drinking Cola. ☐

9. Jeff and Dickson am not watching cartoon. ☐

10. The panda is not dancing. ☐

挑戰站

請參看例子，找出下列現在進行式的句子中的錯誤，並將正確的答案寫在右邊的橫線上。

例子：

Catherine (am no) washing clothes.   is not

Daddy is not (readding) newspaper.   reading

1. Colin is not geting taller. _____

2. Oscar is not driveing a red car. _____

3. Mr. Hui am not talking with Miss Lee. _____

4. We am no having barbecue in Shek O. _____

5. Oliver and Amy are no playying tennis. _____

6. I am not drinkking coffee. _____

7. Brenda is no cookking in the kitchen. _____

8. You is no sitting on the sofa. _____

9. The dog is no running after the boy. _____

10. Chris am no playing football with his classmates. _____

chapter

8

現在進行式：
問句

Present Continuous Tense:
Question Form

　　小忠放學回家，聽到房間裡傳來鋼琴聲，他大聲說：「Is Kathy playing piano?」（是不是凱西在彈琴？）可是沒有人回答他。這時，廚房傳來了一些聲音，小忠又大叫說：「Are mummy and grandma cooking?」（是不是媽媽和祖母在做飯？）仍然沒有人回答他。小忠給弄糊塗了，他一邊自言自語地說：「Am I dreaming?」（我是不是在做夢？）一邊捏一下自己的臉。就在這時，他醒來了，原來剛才在做夢。

　　小忠在夢中所說的話，都運用了現在進行式時態中的問句形式。現在進行式時態中的問句形式主要用來提問、查詢現在進行中的情況或動作。

大家看看以下的時間線圖：

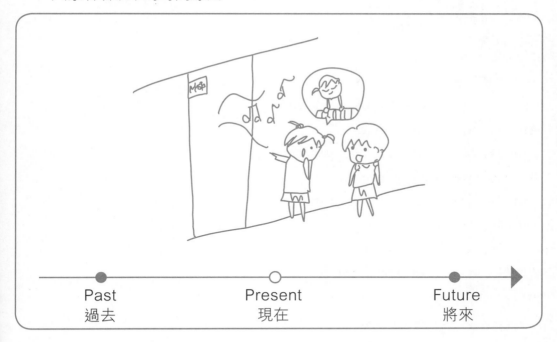

Past 過去　　　　Present 現在　　　　Future 將來

Is Joyce playing piano?
喬伊斯在彈琴嗎？

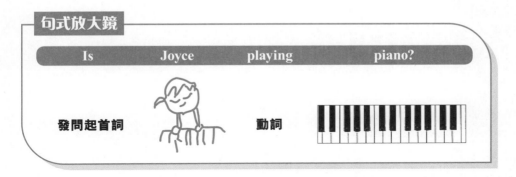

句式放大鏡

| Is | Joyce | playing | piano? |

發問起首詞　　　　　動詞

進行式的問句以be開頭

「Is Joyce playing piano?」是現在進行式的問句形式（The Question Form）。現在進行式的問句形式主要以「be」動詞的現在式「Am」、「Is」、「Are」作為發問起首詞，主詞後面接所提問的動作，即動詞加「ing」。

例如：Am I dreaming?
　　　我在做夢嗎？

　　　Is mummy cooking?
　　　媽媽在做飯嗎？

　　　Is he watching TV?
　　　他在看電視嗎？

Are Tom and Kevin playing football?
湯姆和凱文在踢足球嗎？

Are they having barbecue?
他們在燒烤嗎？

文法加油站

練習一

請將正確的答案圈出來。

例子：Am / Is / (Are) you doing homework?

1. Am / Is / Are I doing wrong?
2. Am / Is / Are Martin and Chris your brothers?
3. Am / Is / Are Joan playing squash?
4. Am / Is / Are the dog drinking water?
5. Am / Is / Are Ken and Patrick watching football match?
6. Am / Is / Are they swimming?
7. Am / Is / Are she drawing a panda?
8. Am / Is / Are we talking to Miss Chan?
9. Am / Is / Are mummy making salad?
10. Am / Is / Are you playing guitar in the room?

練習二

請參看例子，運用提供的字詞，寫出現在進行式的問句。

例子：Alice / listening to / is / music / ?

　　　 Is Alice listening to music?

1. a car / I / drawing / am / ?

_____

2. is / Winnie / talking to / her mother / ?

_____

3. are / washing / Tammy and Peggy / dishes / ?

_____

4. the panda / eating / is / bamboo / ?

_____

5. Kitty and Pat / are / singing / in the music room / ?

_____

6. playing / you / are / chess / with Sam / ?

_____

7. grandpa / watering / is / flowers / in the garden / ?

_____

8. making / am / day dream / I / ?

_____

9. the weather / is / getting / worse / ?

_____

10. watching / is / mummy / TV / in the sitting room / ?

_____

挑戰站

請參看例子，找出下列句子中的錯誤，並將正確的答案寫在右邊的橫線上。

例子：

(Am) Uncle Jason watching TV in the morning?   _____Is_____

Are John and Amy (playeding) piano in the music room?   _____playing_____

Is Miss Fairbrother talking to Amy (!)   _____?_____

1. Am Mike getting taller? _____

2. Are Daisy writing in the room? _____

3. Is Anthony haveing barbecue with his friends? _____

4. Am you talking to Kitty on the phone? _____

5. Is Peter singging in the music room? _____

6. Is Julie listening to music! _____

7. Are Gladys and Connie watched TV in the sitting room? _____

8. Is Mr. Kennedy readding before going to bed? _____

9. Is the bus comeing? _____

10. Are they making sandwiches in the kitchen. _____

chapter 9

現在完成式：
肯定句
Present Perfect Tense: Positive Form

恩恩心愛的小黑狗不見了，她和家人都感到不開心。爸爸説：「I have already patted it.」（我已經輕輕拍過牠。）媽媽説：「I have fed it for many years.」（我已餵飼牠多年了。）弟弟説：「I have played ball game with it.」（我曾跟牠一起玩皮球。）而恩恩自己剛才跟小黑狗説過話，「She has just talked to it.」。究竟小黑狗到了哪裡去呢？

恩恩和她的家人回想跟小黑狗一起的時光時，他們所説的話都運用了現在完成式時態中的肯定句形式。現在完成式時態中的肯定句主要用來表達**剛剛或不久之前已完成的動作、在以前已開始並持續到現在的動作、及在過去已完成的動作，它的影響到現在仍然存在**，以及**曾有的經歷**。恩恩和她的家人所説的話屬於哪一種呢？

38

I have already patted it. ⇨ 不久之前已完成的動作
She has just talked to it. ⇨ 剛剛已完成的動作
I have fed it for many years. ⇨ 在以前已開始並持續到現在的動作
I have played ball game with it. ⇨ 曾有的經歷

大家看看以下的時間線圖：

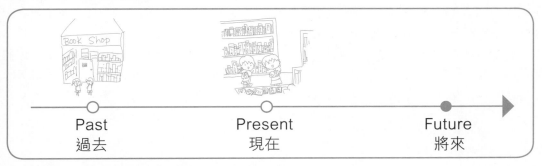

Alice and Juliet have gone to the bookshop.
愛麗斯和茱麗葉已去了書店。（表示她們現在仍在書店）

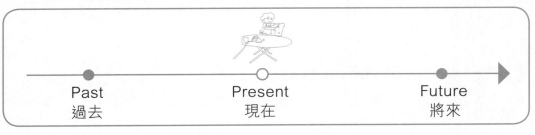

Mummy has already ironed all the clothes.
媽媽剛才已經熨好了所有衣服。

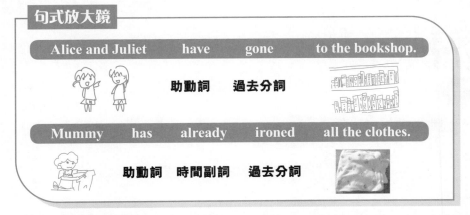

以上兩個句子都是現在完成式的肯定句形式（The Positive Form）。它們都是主詞後接助動詞「have」或「has」，然後接過去分詞。前一句表示在以前已開始並持續到現在的動作，而後一句則表示剛剛或不久之前已完成的動作。而句子該使用「have」或「has」是由主詞決定的。

例如：They have been to Japan.
他們曾經去過日本。
He has lost his weight.
他已減了體重。（表示這個動作在過去已完成，而它的影響到現在仍然存在。）

甚麼時候用現在完成式？

　　大家可有發現「Mummy has already ironed all the clothes.」句中的時間副詞「already」？通常，句中出現「already」（已經）、「just」（剛才）、「yet」（還沒有/有沒有）、「since」（自從）、「for」（已有......時間）、「never」（從沒有/從不）、「ever」（曾/曾經）等字詞時，往往會使用現在完成式。其中「yet」只用於否定句形式，而「ever」用於問句形式。

例如：Frankie has played tennis for five years.　　Benjamin and Ivan have met since 1983.
　　　法蘭基打網球已有五年了。　　　　　　　　自從1983年起，本傑明和伊凡已經認識。
　　　He has just done homework.　　　　　　　She has already eaten a big meal.
　　　他剛剛做了功課。　　　　　　　　　　　她已經吃完了一頓大餐。
　　　I have never been to America.
　　　我不曾去過美國。

　　在現在完成式的句子中，助動詞必須是「have」或「has」的其中一個。怎樣決定該使用哪一個呢？只需留意句中的主詞，如果主詞是「I」、「You」、「They」、「We」、「Sam and Sue」等，就要使用「have」作助動詞；如果主詞是「He」、「She」、「It」、「Sam」等，就要使用「has」作助動詞了。

　　有些動詞的過去分詞是與動詞基本形相同的，例如「put」、「cut」、「cost」、「set」等，有些過去分詞是與動詞基本形完全不同，例如：

動詞基本形	過去分詞
make	made
take	taken
do	done
be	been

文法加油站

練習一

請寫出下列動詞的過去分詞。

動詞基本形	過去分詞	動詞基本形	過去分詞
1. make	_____	9. talk	_____
2. sell	_____	10. put	_____
3. take	_____	11. cut	_____
4. go	_____	12. ride	_____
5. do	_____	13. learn	_____
6. have	_____	14. leave	_____
7. be	_____	15. get	_____
8. sing	_____		

請參看例子,在現在完成式的句子加☑ ,並把句中現在完成式的動詞圈出來,不是的則加上☒。

例子：Miss Chan (has lived) in Hong Kong for ten years.　　☑

1. Dennis and Karen have been good friends for twenty years. ☐

2. Edward always goes to office by MTR. ☐

3. Sidney and Cherry have gone to the library. ☐

4. You have already made a car model. ☐

5. We have never seen a bear before. ☐

6. They are my grandparents. ☐

7. Miss Lee has been Art teacher since 1990. ☐

8. The dog wants some food. ☐

9. The children have just done homework. ☐

10. The train has just left. ☐

挑戰站

請將正確的答案寫在橫線上。

1. She _____ (be) a mother since 2001.

2. He _____ never_____ (play) guitar.

3. I _____ (live) in France for five years.

4. Martin _____ (learn) English for two years.

5. Kitty and Sandy _____ just _____ (come) back from China.

6. Joey and Kelly _____ (be) good friends since 2000.

7. We _____ (put) the old clothes to the recycle box already.

8. Mr. Lam _____ (manage) the company since 1982.

9. You _____ (work) for this company for three years.

10. Grandpa _____already_____ (mend) the bike for me.

chapter 10

現在完成式：否定句

Present Perfect Tense: Negative Form

　　恩恩的小黑狗仍未回家，令她非常擔心。恩恩和弟弟做起小偵探來，四出查問周圍的鄰居有沒有見過小黑狗。大廈保安員說：「I have not seen it.」（我不曾見過牠。）住在隔壁的小明說：「I have not played with it.」（我不曾跟牠玩過。）究竟小黑狗到了哪裡呢？

　　大廈保安員和小明所說的話，都運用了現在完成式時態中的否定句形式。現在完成式時態中的否定句主要用來否定**剛剛或不久之前已完成的動作**、**在以前已開始並持續到現在的動作**，以及**曾有的經歷**。

大家看看以下的時間線圖：

The children have not done their homework yet.
孩子們不曾做完功課。

句式放大鏡

The children	have	not	done	their homework	yet.

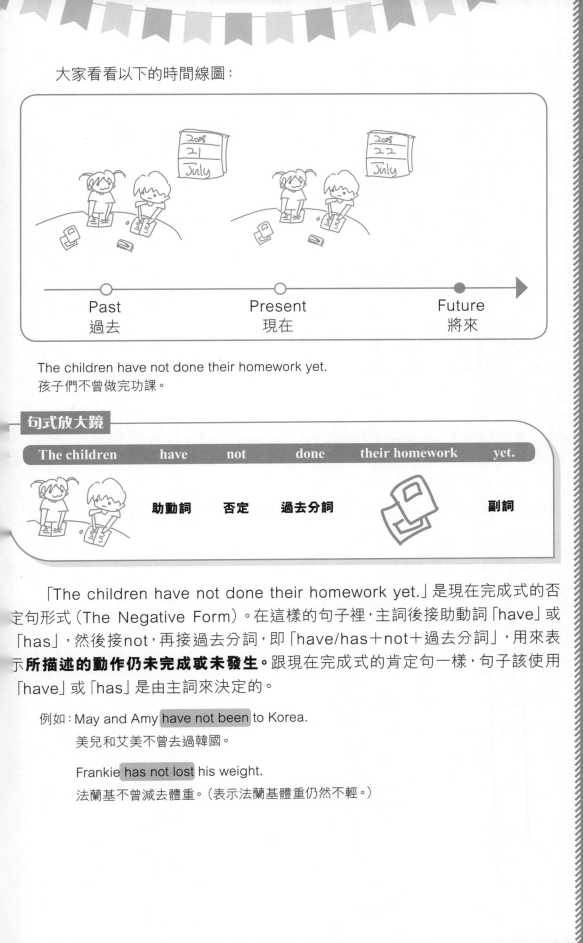

助動詞　　否定　　過去分詞　　　　　　　　　　副詞

「The children have not done their homework yet.」是現在完成式的否定句形式（The Negative Form）。在這樣的句子裡，主詞後接助動詞「have」或「has」，然後接not，再接過去分詞，即「have/has＋not＋過去分詞」，用來表示**所描述的動作仍未完成或未發生。**跟現在完成式的肯定句一樣，句子該使用「have」或「has」是由主詞來決定的。

例如：May and Amy have not been to Korea.
　　　美兒和艾美不曾去過韓國。

　　　Frankie has not lost his weight.
　　　法蘭基不曾減去體重。（表示法蘭基體重仍然不輕。）

當句中出現yet的時候

大家留意句中的副詞「yet」（還沒有/有沒有），當句中出現這個字詞時，往往會使用現在完成式的否定句形式。另外，留意「yet」也可用於問句形式。

例如：Francis has not gone to the library yet.
法朗西斯仍未去圖書館。

He has not made the car model yet.
他仍未砌好汽車模型。

Grandma has not slept yet.
祖母仍未睡覺。

文法加油站

練習一

請參看例子，在現在完成式的否定句上加 ☑，不是現在完成式的否定句上加 ☒。

例子：Joan is not my cousin.   ☒
      He has not done his homework.   ☑

1. Dianna and Ann were not in the same class last year. ☐

2. Jason has not gone to supermarket. ☐

3. I have not lived in America. ☐

4. You are not playing football now. ☐

5. We have not had a barbecue in Lamma Island. ☐

6. They are not my sisters. ☐

7. He has not been a doctor. ☐

8. We do not want some sandwiches. ☐

9. The dog has not run after the cat. ☐

10. Uncle Dick has not seen us for many years. ☐

請將正確的答案寫在橫線上。

ring	play	be	make	leave
water	study	finish	receive	buy

1. The girl has not _____ France.

2. The children have not _____ football.

3. Mary and John have not _____ in America.

4. We have not _____ the model yet.

5. Grandma has not _____ the flowers.

6. Joey has not _____ talking on the phone.

7. The door bell has not _____.

8. I have not _____ your email.

9. The ferry has not _____ the pier.

10. You have not _____ the ticket yet!

挑戰站

請參看例子，找出下列現在完成式否定句中的錯誤，並將正確的答案寫在右邊的橫線上。

例子：

Cathy (have) not washed all the clothes.	has
They have (no saw) him for many years.	not seen

1. Alan has no finishhed talking to Mary on the phone. _____

2. Oliver and Kerry has not done their homework. _____

3. Mr. Leung has not work for this company. _____

4. You has no buy the ticket. _____

5. Amy have not played computer game yet. _____

6. I has not had lunch yet. _____

7. Belinda has not make salad yet. _____

8. We have no sleep. _____

9. The train has not arrive yet. _____

10. Faye have no read this book. _____

chapter
11

現在完成式：問句

Present Perfect Tense: Question Form

恩恩決定到公園去找小黑狗，她問老伯伯：「Have you ever seen my dog?」（你曾見過我的狗嗎？）她又問一個經常餵飼流浪狗的嬸嬸：「Have you fed my dog?」（你曾餵飼過我的狗嗎？）又問了一個愛狗的叔叔：「Have you played with my dog?」（你有沒有跟我的狗玩？）找了大半天，還是找不到，老伯伯關心地說：「Has the dog gone home yet?」（小狗還沒有回家嗎？）。

恩恩和老伯伯所說的話，都運用了現在完成式時態中的問句形式。現在完成式時態中的問句形式主要用來**提問或查詢動作是否已經完成，或事情是否已經發生**。

大家看看以下的時間線圖：

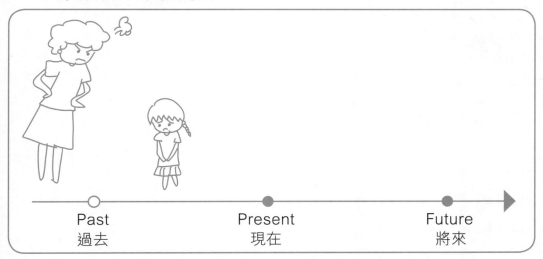

Have you ever done your homework?
你已經做完了功課嗎？

「Have you ever done your homework?」是現在完成式的問句形式（The Question Form）。現在完成式的問句形式的發問起首詞是「Have」或「Has」，後接主詞，然後接過去分詞，表示說話的人提問或查詢動作是否完成了，或事情曾否發生了。

例如：Have Anna and Henry been to Paris?　　Has she seen him?
　　　安娜和亨利已去過巴黎嗎？　　　　　她已見過他嗎？

出現ever和yet時

大家可有留意句中的副詞「ever」（曾/曾經）？「ever」通常用於現在完成式的問句形式，一般緊接主詞後面；另一個副詞「yet」（還沒有/有沒有）也可用於現在完成式的問句形式，通常出現在句末。

例如：Has Danny come yet?　　　　　　　Have they ever seen each other?
　　　丹尼已經來了沒有？　　　　　　　他們曾經見過面嗎？

文法加油站

練習一

請將正確的答案圈出來。

例子：Has / (Have) Peter and Tom been late?

　　　(Has) / Have it come home yet?

1. Has / Have Mr. Smith been a fireman?

2. Has / Have the train left the platform yet?

3. Has / Have they bought the books?

4. Has / Have Tommy gone hiking with his friends?

5. Has / Have the children finished the game yet?

6. Has / Have Grace ever seen Mr. Chan?

7. Has / Have you ever found my dog?

8. Has / Have Sean studied in France?

9. Has / Have you ever been to Beijing?

10. Has / Have Miff cleaned her room yet?

練習二

請參看例子，運用提供的字詞，寫出現在完成式問句。

例子：been / a firewoman / Has / Lily / ?

　　　Has Lily been a firewoman?

1. finished / they / Have / the dinner / yet / ?

_____

2. Jessica and Vincent / left / Have / yet / ?

_____

3. ever / she / seen / Has / this movie / ?

_____

4. made / Have / they / the model / yet / ?

_____

5. in Kowloon Bay / lived / Ken and Amy / Have / ?

_____

6. Francis and you / in the same class / been / Have / ever / ?

_____

7. you / played / Have / with my dog / ?

_____

8. made / a pizza / mummy / Has / ever / ?

_____

9. Hong Kong / Has / a fishing village / been / ?

_____

10. the children / yet / done / Have / their homework / ?

_____

挑戰站

請參看例子，找出下列句子中的錯誤，並將正確的答案寫在右邊的橫線上。

例子：

(Have) Mandy sent the letter yet?   Has

Have June and Henry (went) to Shatin?   gone

1. Has Henry be a singer?   _____

2. Have Tracy and Pat go out yet?   _____

3. Has Andy ever find his bag?   _____

4. Have Shirley and Amy clean their room yet?   _____

5. Have they dance for the party?   _____

6. Has Chris saw the old man?   _____

7. Has Colin and Jacky traveled Africa?   _____

8. Has you worked in Russia?   _____

9. Have you finish drawing yet?   _____

10. Have Raymond washed the dishes yet?   _____

chapter 12

簡單過去式：
肯定句

Simple Past Tense:
Positive Form

　　假期後，盈盈對芳芳説：「I visited my grandma in Tai Po. My grandma was a doctor in the past. My family and I stayed at grandma's home for a few days. We had a happy holiday there.」（我探望了祖母。我的祖母以前是醫生。我和家人在祖母家住了數天。我們在那兒過了一個愉快的假期。）

　　盈盈所説的話運用了過去式時態中的肯定句形式。過去式時態中的肯定句形式主要用來描述**過去的情況或狀態，即過去做了的事情**。

大家看看以下的時間線圖：

Past   Present   Future
過去   現在   將來

問：What did your grandma do in the past?
以前你的祖母做甚麼工作？

答：My grandma was a doctor in the past.
以前我的祖母是醫生。

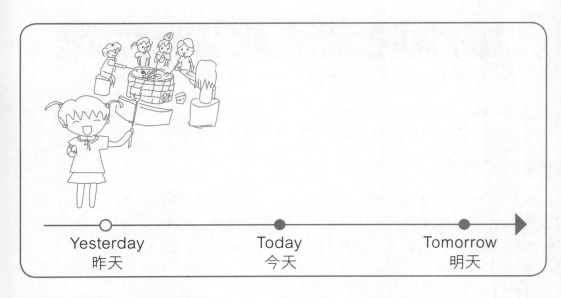

Yesterday   Today   Tomorrow
昨天   今天   明天

問：What did Alice do yesterday?
昨天愛麗斯做了甚麼？

答：Alice had barbecue yesterday.
昨天愛麗斯去燒烤了。

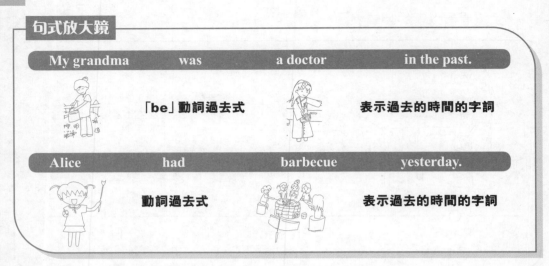

句式放大鏡

| My grandma | was | a doctor | in the past. |

「be」動詞過去式　　　　表示過去的時間的字詞

| Alice | had | barbecue | yesterday. |

動詞過去式　　　　　表示過去的時間的字詞

　　「My grandma was a doctor in the past.」和「Alice had barbecue yesterday.」是過去式的肯定句形式（The Positive Form），大家留意句子裡的動詞「was」和「had」都是動詞過去式。

　　我們先來說明前一個句子。前一個句子中的動詞「was」是「be」動詞中的「is」的過去式。大家看看以下的比較表：

主語	動詞基本形	現在式	過去式
I, He, She, It	be	am, is	was
We, You, They	be	are	were

was和were

　　在表示過去式的句子裡，當主詞是「I」、「He」、「She」、「It」、「Kerry」、「Sharon」時，動詞必須使用「was」；當主詞「We」、「You」、「They」、「Kerry and Sharon」時，動詞必須使用「were」。

例如：My grandpa was sixty years old last year.
　　　去年我的祖父六十歲。

　　　Sharon and Kathy were in the same class in the past.
　　　以前莎倫和凱西是同一班的。

至於後一個句子，在過去式的句子裡，當動詞是一般動詞（即不是「be」動詞）時，無論主詞是「I」、「We」、「You」、「They」、「Peter and Joe」，還是「He」、「She」、「It」、「Kathy」、「Jason」等，只要句子所表達的時間是過去了的或所描述的動作已發生了，動詞必須使用過去式。

例如：Kelly played basketball with her classmates yesterday.
昨天嘉莉和同學打籃球。

They went hiking last week.
上星期他們去了行山。

表示過去的時間字詞

一般來説，描述過去發生的事情、行為、想法時，句中通常都有一些表示過去的時間字詞，如ago（之前）、yesterday（昨天）、last week（上星期）、last Monday（上星期一）、last month（上個月）、last year（去年）、in the past（以前）等等。所以，當我們在句中看到這些字詞時，就知道這個句子所表達的時態是過去式。

例如：

Simon studied in Japan a few years ago.
多年前西門在日本讀書。

Sharon and I went to swim yesterday.
昨天莎倫和我去了游泳。

Mummy made a chocolate cake last week.
上星期媽媽做了一個巧克力蛋糕。

Uncle Peter was teacher in the past.
彼得叔叔以前是老師。

> 大家仍記得甚麼是不規則動詞（Irregular Verbs）嗎？在英語裡，有一些動詞的過去式（Past Tense）和過去分詞（Past Participle）跟動詞基本形是不同的，這些動詞就稱為不規則動詞，例如「make」是動詞基本形，它的過去式是「made」，過去分詞也是「made」；又例如「see」是動詞基本形，它的過去式是「saw」，過去分詞是「seen」。

文法加油站

練習一

請參看例子，在過去式的句子加 ☑，並把句中過去式的動詞圈出來，不是的則加 ☒。

例子：Jessica (studied) in America a few years ago.　☑

1. Danny and Kitty were in the same class last year.　☐
2. Jason goes to school by bus.　☐
3. I am ten years old now.　☐
4. You played football yesterday.　☐
5. We had a barbecue in Shek O last Sunday.　☐
6. They are my sisters.　☐
7. He was a teacher in the past.　☐
8. We want some Cola.　☐
9. It was rainy last night.　☐
10. Mummy made some sandwiches last week.　☐

練習二

請將正確的答案寫在橫線上。

1. The boy _____ (be) four years old two years ago.
2. The children _____ (have) a barbecue last weekend.
3. My uncle _____ (be) a lawyer in the past.
4. We _____ (win) the game yesterday.
5. He _____ (put) the book on the desk last night.
6. Joyce and Kitty _____ (see) an exciting movie last Sunday.
7. I _____ (help) mummy cleaning the room last week.
8. It _____ (be) sunny yesterday.
9. You_____ (dress) up as a wizard at Halloween last year.
10. They _____ (go) to Italy last winter.

這是艾美的記事本,請細心觀看下面的內容,並參看例子,把她上星期做過的事情寫下來。

2nd - 8th May, 2020	
Monday	Have swimming class after school.
Tuesday	Help grandpa watering flowers.
	Play piano at home.
Wednesday	Help mummy making a chocolate cake.
	Have a story time with mummy before going to bed.
Thursday	Have a walk with grandpa after dinner.
Friday	Visit Aunt Sharon at 6:00PM.
	Play computer game with my cousin at Aunt Sharon's home.
Saturday	Go to Hong Kong Disneyland with daddy and mummy.
Sunday	Clean my room.
	Have dinner with my family at Sun Sun Restaurant.

例句:Amy had swimming class after school last Monday.

1. Amy _____ .

2. _____ .

3. _____ .

4. _____ .

5. _____ .

6. _____ .

7. _____ .

8. _____ .

9. _____ .

10. _____ .

小學生學 *Grammar* ——句子文法

55

chapter 13

簡單過去式：否定句

Simple Past Tense: Negative Form

小明問小樂週末做了甚麼事情。小樂故意作弄小明，說：「The weather was not good last weekend.」（上個週末天氣不好。）「I did not wake up at six o'clock.」（我沒有在六時起床。）「My brother and I did not hurry up for school bus.（弟弟和我不用匆匆忙忙地趕校巴。）We did not go to school last weekend.（我們上週末不用上學。）哈哈⋯⋯」誰都知道週末不用上學！小明真是給小樂氣死了！

小樂跟小明所說的話，是運用了過去式時態中的否定形式。過去式時態中的否定形式主要用來**否定過去的情況或狀態**。

大家看看以下的時間線圖：

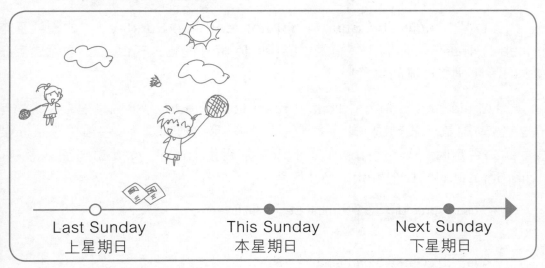

Last Sunday	This Sunday	Next Sunday
上星期日	本星期日	下星期日

問：Did Annie and Sharon read last Sunday?
　　上星期日安妮和莎倫看書了嗎？

答：Annie and Sharon did not read last Sunday.
　　上星期日安妮和莎倫沒有看書。

問：Was the weather cloudy last Sunday?
　　上星期日是陰天嗎？

答：The weather was not cloudy last Sunday.
　　上星期日不是陰天。

句式放大鏡

Annie and Sharon	did	not	read	last Sunday.
	助動詞	否定	動詞基本形	表示過去的時間的字詞

The weather	was	not	cloudy	last Sunday.
	動詞	否定		表示過去的時間的字詞

「Annie and Sharon did not read last Sunday.」和「The weather was not cloudy last Sunday.」都是過去式的否定句形式（The Negative Form）。

助動詞 did not

大家留意「Annie and Sharon did not read last Sunday.」中的動詞基本形「read」前面有「did not」。這是助動詞「do not」的過去式否定式，表示否定在過去的時態裡所描述的事情。

在「Annie and Sharon did not read last Sunday.」這個過去否定式的句子裡，當動詞是一般動詞（即不是「be」動詞）時，動詞是不受主詞影響的。要表示過去否定時，只需使用助動詞「did」加否定「not」，後接動詞基本形，如「did not read」、「did not have」等等。

例如：The children did not go to the beach last week.
上星期孩子們不是去沙灘。

We did not have a barbecue last Saturday.
上星期六我們沒有燒烤。

I did not see this movie a few days ago.
數天前我不是看這部電影。

She did not water the flowers last night.
昨晚她不是淋花。

was not 和 were not

而「The weather was not cloudy last Sunday.」中的動詞「was」後面接「not」，也是具有否定在過去的時態裡所描述的事情的意思。

大家觀看並比較以下這個表：

主語	動詞基本形	現在否定式	過去否定式
I, He, She, It	be + not	am not, is not	was not
We, You, They	be + not	are not	were not

在表示過去否定的句子裡，當主詞是單數，即「I」、「He」、「She」、「It」、「Ken」、「Stella」時，動詞必須使用「was not」；當主詞是複數，即「We」、「You」、「They」、「Ken and Stella」、「The children」時，動詞必須使用「were not」。

例如：I was not eleven years old last year.
去年我不是十一歲。

Cathy and Judy were not in the same class in the past.
以前凱西和茱迪不是同一班的。

!　「was not」、「were not」的縮寫分別是「wasn't」和「weren't」。而「did not」的縮寫是「didn't」。

文法加油站

練習一

請參看例子，在過去式的否定形式句子加 ☑，並把句中的否定式圈出來，不是的則加 ☒。

例子：He (was not) a librarian in the past. ☑

1. Alan and Alice were in the same class last year. ☐

2. They were not my brothers. ☐

3. I was not three years old. ☐

4. You did not go to swim last week. ☐

5. We did not have a barbecue last month. ☐

6. She was a teacher. ☐

7. He was not a doctor in the past. ☐

8. She did not see him last summer. ☐

9. The weather was not good yesterday. ☐

10. The dog did not eat anything last night. ☐

練習二

請將正確的答案寫在橫線上。

1. We _____ (be not) in the same class last year.

2. Mr. Leung _____ (not dress) up as a deer at Christmas last year.

3. She _____ (be not) a teacher in the past.

4. The dog _____ (not sleep) under the chair last night.

5. Greg _____ (not make) a blueberry cake for her mother last year.

6. Anson and Jack _____ (not see) each other two years ago.

7. Benson _____ (not go) to Taiwan last winter.

8. It _____ (be not) a sunny day yesterday.

9. I _____ (be not) a fat boy in the past.

10. They _____ (not watch) TV last night.

挑戰站

請參看例子，運用提供的字詞，寫出過去式否定式的句子。

例子：Abbie / ride / in the park / a bicycle / did not / .
　　　Abbie did not ride a bicycle in the park.

1. Jacky and Stella / in Hong Kong / were / not / last week / .

_____

2. was / Miss Lee / not / a teacher / in the past / .

_____

3. did / I / watch / the football match / last night / not / .

_____

4. You / not / attend / the swimming class / did / last Monday / .

_____

5. We / make / did / a model / not / a few days ago / .

_____

6. did / The children / play / not / a few hours ago / chess / .

_____

7. The cat / go / did / home / not / yesterday / .

_____

8. Tim / see / the accident / did / not / last night / .

_____

9. were / not / Ben and Eric / last year / in the same class / .

_____

10. Francis / put / did / not / the glasses on the table / a few hours ago / .

_____

chapter 14

簡單過去式：問句

Simple Past Tense: Question Form

　　環遊世界多年的叔叔終於回來了，美兒對叔叔的遊歷很感興趣，於是纏着叔叔問個不停：「Did you go to Africa?」（你去過非洲嗎？）「Did you see koala?」（你見過樹熊嗎？）「Was this kiwi born in New Zealand?」（這隻幾維鳥是在新西蘭出生的嗎？）「Did you travel Tibet?」（你去了西藏嗎？）美兒一連串的問題，令叔叔一時答不過來。

　　美兒問叔叔的問題，都運用了過去式時態中的問句形式。過去式時態中的問句形式主要用來**提問、查詢過去的情況或狀態，以及過去發生的事情。**

大家看看以下的時間線圖：

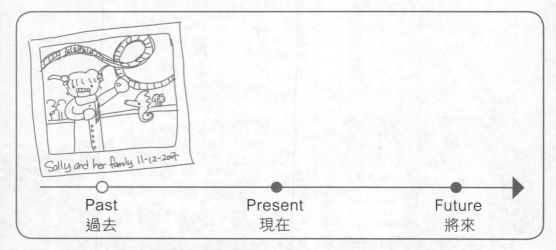

Past	Present	Future
過去	現在	將來

Did Sally go to the Ocean Park last winter?　　Was she happy?
去年冬天莎莉去了海洋公園嗎？　　她覺得開心嗎？

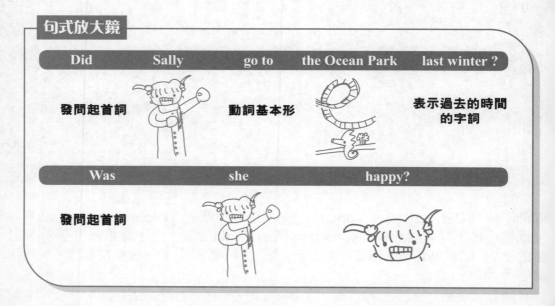

句式放大鏡

Did	**Sally**	**go to**	**the Ocean Park**	**last winter ?**
發問起首詞		**動詞基本形**		**表示過去的時間的字詞**

Was	**she**	**happy?**
發問起首詞		

「Did Sally go to the Ocean Park last winter?」和「Was she happy?」是過去式的問句形式（The Question Form），前一句是以助動詞「did」為發問起首詞，後一句是以「be」動詞的過去式為發問起首詞。大家留意這兩句的發問起首詞「Did」和「Was」是過去式問句中其中兩種發問的形式，即以助動詞「Did」和「be」動詞的過去式「Was」、「Were」作為發問的起首詞。

以did作發問起首詞

在過去式的問句裡，任何主詞都可以以助動詞「did」作發問起首詞；而以「did」作發問起首詞後，描述有關動作的動詞必須是基本形。

以「be」動詞的過去式作發問起首詞，當主詞是「I」、「He」、「She」、「It」、「Tony」、「Daddy」時，發問起首詞必須是「Was」；當主詞是「You」、「We」、「They」、「Mary and Lily」時，發問起首詞必須是「Were」。

例如：Did daddy and mummy get married in 1974?
爸爸和媽媽在1974年結婚嗎？

Did you go to Thailand last summer?
去年夏天你去了泰國嗎？

Was I young and beautiful in the past?
我以前年輕漂亮嗎？

Was Tommy a taxi driver a few years ago?
數年前湯米是計程車司機嗎？

Were they happy in America a few years ago?
數年前他們在美國快樂嗎？

文法加油站

練習一

請將正確的答案圈出來。

例子：Did / Was / (Were) they late yesterday?
　　　(Did) / Was / Were he come last night?

1. Did / Was / Were Dicky a fireman a few years ago?

2. Did / Was / Were you make an apple pie yesterday?

3. Did / Was / Were he handsome when he was young?

4. Did / Was / Were Mary and Kelly go hiking last Sunday?

5. Did / Was / Were the children play computer game last night?

6. Did / Was / Were Grace dance last weekend?

7. Did / Was / Were mummy go to market a few hours ago?

8. Did / Was / Were Simon and Sean happy in America a few years ago?

9. Did / Was / Were Mrs. Wong live in Hong Kong Island in the past?

10. Did / Was / Were Mr. Poon a postman in the past?

練習二

請參看例子，運用提供的字詞，寫出過去式問句。

例子：a lawyer / was / Mr. Wong / in the past / ?
　　　Was Mr. Wong a lawyer in the past?

1. late / he / was / yesterday / ?

_____

2. Judy / go home / did / at eleven o'clock / ?

_____

3. they / see / did / a movie / last week / ?

_____

4. a beautiful lady / was / grandma / when she was young / ?

_____

5. a few years ago / in Tai Po / live / Ken / did / ?

_____

6. Tammy and you / in the same class / were / last year / ?

_____

7. a panda / draw / did / Susan / a few hours ago / ?

_____

8. make / an apple pie / mummy / did / last night / ?

_____

9. cloudy / was / the weather / last Sunday / ?

_____

10. the children / fight / did / yesterday / ?

_____

挑戰站

請參看例子，找出下列句子中的錯誤，並將正確的答案寫在右邊的橫線上。

例子：Did Mr. Lee (posted) the letter yesterday?   _____post_____

(Was) June and Kelly go to Shatin?   _____Did_____

(Did) they late last night?   _____Were_____

1. Were Henry ten years old last year?   _____

2. Was Pat go to the museum yesterday?   _____

3. Did Anthony made a model last Sunday?   _____

4. Did Sue fat in the past?   _____

5. Did he a dancer a few years ago?   _____

6. Were Chris late yesterday?   _____

7. Did Connie and Joyce in the same class last year?   _____

8. Was you work in Japan a few years ago?   _____

9. Were you read this book last week?   _____

10. Was Ray do homework yesterday?   _____

chapter 15

過去進行式：肯定句

Past Continuous Tense: Positive Form

峰峰和方方談起昨天做的事情。峰峰說：「I was doing homework at 2:00PM yesterday.」（昨天下午二時我正在做功課。）「I was playing computer game when you phoned me.」（當你打電話給我時，我正在玩電腦遊戲。）

峰峰告訴方方昨天某段時間正在做甚麼事情，他所說的話運用了過去進行式時態中的肯定句形式。過去進行式時態中的肯定句形式主要**用來描述在過去某段時間裡，正在進行中的動作**。

大家看看以下的時間線圖：

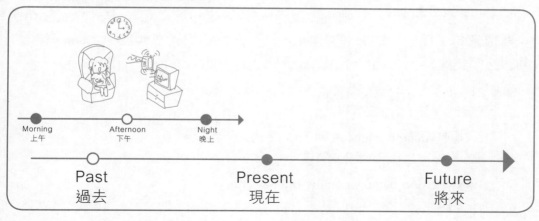

問：What was Sally doing at 3:00PM yesterday?

　　昨天下午三時莎莉正在做甚麼？

答：Sally was watching TV at 3:00PM yesterday.

　　昨天下午三時莎莉正在看電視。

問：What was Sally doing when the phone rang?

　　當電話響起時，莎莉正在做甚麼？

答：Sally was watching TV when the phone rang.

　　當電話響起時，莎莉正在看電視。

句式放大鏡

Sally	was	watching	TV	at 3:00PM yesterday.
	動詞	動詞+ing		表示過去某時段的字詞

Sally	was	watching	TV	when the phone rang.
	動詞	動詞+ing		表示過去某時段 另一事情發生了

「Sally was watching TV at 3:00PM yesterday.」和「Sally was watching TV when the phone rang.」，是過去進行式的肯定句形式（The Positive Form）。大家要留意句子裡的動詞必須是「was」、「were」的其中一個，而描述有關動作的動詞必須在尾部加「ing」，例如「watching」、「reading」、「playing」等等。

例如：The children were playing games at noon yesterday.
　　　昨天中午孩子們正在玩遊戲。

He was doing homework when Uncle John came.
當約翰叔叔來時，他正在做功課。

I was playing piano when the phone rang.
當電話響起時，我正在彈琴。

表示過去時段的字詞

在過去進行式的句子裡，通常會有表示過去某時段的字詞，如「at 3:00PM yesterday」。它跟過去式句子裡表示時間的字詞不同的地方是，過去式句子裡表示時間的字詞沒有特別指明某個時段，但過去進行式的句子通常都有指明某時段的字詞，如「at noon yesterday」、「at 10:00PM last night」等等。

例如：My brother was playing football at noon yesterday.
　　　昨天中午我的弟弟正在踢足球。

They were drawing at 2:00PM last Sunday.
上星期天下午二時他們正在畫畫。

另外，當句中出現一些連接詞，如「when」、「while」、「as」時，通常前一個動作會使用過去進行式，而後一個較短、較快的動作會使用過去式。

例如：Sally was watching TV（過去進行式）when the phone rang（過去式）.

It was raining（過去進行式）while Kelly got（過去式）up.
當嘉莉起床時，正在下雨。

The children were playing（過去進行式）chess as daddy went（過去式）out.
當爸爸出門時，孩子們正在下棋。

> ❗ 當主詞是「I」、「He」、「She」、「It」、「David」時，動詞必須使用「was」；當主詞是「We」、「You」、「They」、「David and Sandy」時，動詞必須使用「were」。

文法加油站

練習一

在過去進行式肯定句形式的句子上加 ☑，不是的則加上 ☒。

1. Kerry and Miff were playing tennis at 10:00AM yesterday. ☐

2. Mummy was cooking while I came home. ☐

3. I go to school by bus. ☐

4. You are sleeping when the phone rang. ☐

5. We had a barbecue last week. ☐

6. They were watching TV at 2:00PM yesterday. ☐

7. Look! The bus is coming. ☐

8. She was drawing as daddy went out. ☐

9. Johnny was shouting at you when you crossed the road. ☐

10. Adrian put the book on the desk yesterday. ☐

練習二

請參看例子，找出下列過去進行式句子的錯誤，並將正確的答案寫在橫線上。

例子：1. Kitty (were done) homework at 6:00PM yesterday.   was doing

        2. Mummy was cooking while I (come) home.   came

1. Penny were playing piano at 4:00PM yesterday. _____

2. Grandma was watchhing TV while I went out. _____

3. I was writing when you ring me. _____

4. Mandy was readding when her daddy went out . _____

5. We was haveing a barbecue at 2:00PM yesterday. _____

6. Daddy and mummy was watching TV at 2:00AM last night. _____

7. It was raining when I meet you. _____

8. They was playing tennis at 5:00PM yesterday. _____

9. Johnson was working when I see him. _____

10. Annie and Tom was talkking while she came. _____

過去進行式：肯定句　Past Continuous Tense : Positive Form

挑戰站

請參看例子，利用連接詞「when」、「while」或「as」寫出過去進行式的肯定句。

例子：The phone rang.　　　　　　John was writing.
　　　John was writing when the phone rang.

1. Peter was sleeping.　　　　　　The theft entered his house.

_____

2. The door bell rang.　　　　　　Paul and Jimmy were making model.

_____

3. Mrs. Cheung was writing.　　　　Mr. Cheung came home.

_____

4. Sally came.　　　　　　　　　　We were playing computer game.

_____

5. Tom was drawing.　　　　　　　His grandma went out.

_____

6. I was walking.　　　　　　　　The accident happened.

_____

7. Tammy and Elsa were swimming.　It rained.

_____

8. Aunt Amy visited.　　　　　　　You were sleeping.

_____

9. I was eating.　　　　　　　　　The phone rang.

_____

10. Daddy was having breakfast.　　I woke up.

_____

過去進行式：
否定句
Past Continuous Tense: Negative Form

美尼問東尼昨天下午在做甚麼，東尼故意作弄她，説：「I was not doing homework in the afternoon yesterday. I was not reading. I was not playing.」美尼知道東尼在作弄她，生氣地説：「你昨天下午到底在做甚麼？！」

東尼對美尼所説的話採用了甚麼時態呢？它們又屬於哪一種句子形式？其實，他所説的話是過去進行式時態中的否定句形式。當我們想描述**在過去某段時間裡不在進行中的動作時**，可以使用過去進行式時態中的否定句形式。

過去進行式：否定句 Past Continuous Tense : Negative Form

大家看看以下的時間線圖：

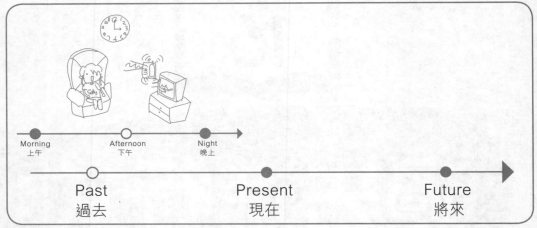

問：Was Sally watching TV at 4:00PM yesterday?
　　昨天下午四時莎莉正在看電視嗎？

答：No, Sally was not watching TV at 4:00PM yesterday.
　　不，昨天下午四時莎莉不是在看電視。

問：Was Sally watching TV when the phone rang?
　　當電話響起時，莎莉正在看電視嗎？

答：No, Sally was not watching TV when the phone rang.
　　不，當電話響起時，莎莉不是在看電視。

句式放大鏡

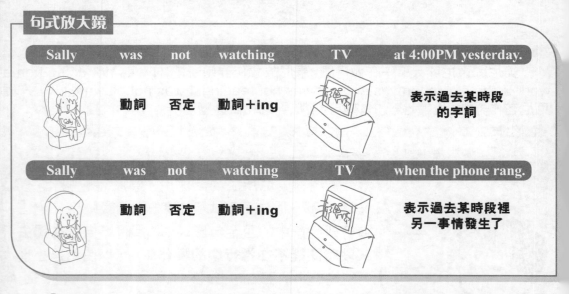

「Sally was not watching TV at 4:00PM yesterday.」和「Sally was no
watching TV when the phone rang.」是過去進行式的否定句形式（The
Negative Form）。提一提大家要留意句子裡的動詞必須是「was」、「were」的
其中一個，然後接「not」，即「was＋not」、「were＋not」，然後才接描述有關動
作的動詞＋ing，例如「was not watching」、「were not reading」、「were no
playing」等等。

例如：They were not playing table tennis at noon yesterday.
昨天中午他們不是在打乒乓球。

Kenney was not making model while the door bell rang.
當門鈴響起時，肯尼不是在做模型。

When the phone rang, I was not washing dishes.
當電話響起時，我不是在洗碗。

文法加油站

練習一

請參看例子，利用提供的字詞，寫出過去進行式的否定句形式的句子。

例子：Julie / riding / was / not / at noon yesterday / .
　　　Julie was not riding at noon yesterday.

1. Sam and May / watching TV / at 9:00PM last night / were / not / .

_____

2. Uncle Ray / reading / in the afternoon yesterday / was / not / .

_____

3. I / doing / homework / was / while / not / daddy came home / .

_____

4. Amy and you / playing / tennis / when it rained / were / not / .

_____

5. Simon / making / when I saw him / car model / was / not / .

_____

6. Mummy / washing / dishes / was / not / at 8:00PM last night / .

_____

7. The dog / sleeping / when I came home / was / not / .

_____

8. Benny and Kitty / making / sandwiches / were / not / at noon yesterday / .

_____

9. were / not / Tammy and Eric / singing / at 12:00PM last night / .

_____

10. Brenda / shopping / was / not / when the accident happened / .

_____

練習二

請在正確的句子上加 ☑，錯誤的句子上加 ☒。

1. The dog were not running. ☐

2. Pat and Danny were not playing badminton at 2:00PM yesterday. ☐

3. Mr. Fong was not reading when the door bell rang . ☐

4. When Nancy phoned me, I was not playing chess. ☐

5. Tommy were not sleeping at 9:00PM last night. ☐

6. Mummy was talking to Mrs. Lee when daddy came home. ☐

7. Joe and Joey was not cooking at 7:00PM yesterday. ☐

8. You were not drawing while the phone rang. ☐

9. When it rained, Jeff and David was not talking. ☐

10. The panda was not eating while I visited it. ☐

挑戰站

請參看例子，找出下列現在進行式的句子中的錯誤，並將正確的答案寫在右邊的橫線上。

例子：Kathy is no washing clothes at noon yesterday.   was not

       Mr. Wong was not readding newspaper as the door bell rang.   reading

1. Colin is not talking to Sam while I saw him. _____

2. Connie was no driveing when the accident happened. _____

3. Rebecca were not watching TV at 4:00PM yesterday. _____

4. They was no having barbecue when it rained. _____

5. Kelly and Jason was no playying computer game at 2:00PM
yesterday. _____

6. I were not doing homework when Uncle Simon came. _____

7. Betty was no cooking as the phone rang. _____

8. He were no playing football at 6:00PM yesterday. _____

9. The dog was no runing after the cat when I saw it. _____

10. Chris was not sleepping at 11:00PM last night. _____

過去進行式：問句

Past Continuous Tense: Question Form

昨晚十二時，有小偷來了叔叔的家，偷了一些東西。警員來了解情況，同時查問了屋內所有的人。警員問叔叔：「Was you sleeping at 12:00PM last night?」（昨晚十二時你在睡覺嗎？）又問嬸嬸：「Was you sleeping when the theft entered your house?」（當小偷進來時，你在睡覺嗎？）。

你們知道警員提問的句式屬於哪個時態和哪種句式嗎？其實，他所說的話運用了過去進行式時態中的問句形式。過去進行式時態中的問句形式主要用來**提問、查詢在過去某段時間裡正在進行中的情況或動作**。

大家看看以下的時間線圖：

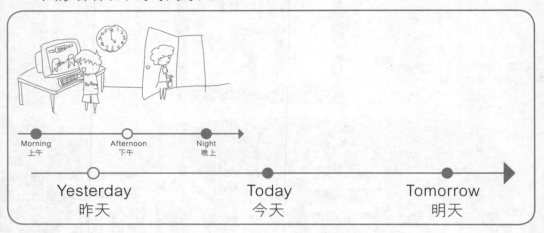

Was Anthony playing computer game at 5:00PM yesterday?
昨天下午五時安東尼正在玩電腦遊戲嗎？

Was Anthony playing computer game when mummy went out?
媽媽出門時，安東尼正在玩電腦遊戲嗎？

句式放大鏡

「Was Anthony playing computer game at 5:00PM yesterday?」和「Was Anthony playing computer game when mummy went out?」都是過去進行式的問句（The Question Form）。過去進行式的問句主要以「be」動詞的過去式「Was」、「Were」作為發問起首詞，主詞後面接提問的動作，即動詞加「ing」。

例如：Was he sleeping while the theft entered his house?
　　　當小偷進來時，他正在睡覺嗎？

　　　Were daddy and mummy talking at 11:00PM last night?
　　　昨晚十一時爸爸和媽媽正在談話嗎？

文法加油站

練習一

請將正確的答案圈出來。

例子： Was / (Were) you doing homework at 3:00PM yesterday?

1. Was / Were Judy sleeping when the theft entered her house?

2. Was / Were Mandy and Ken singing while the phone rang?

3. Was / Were Miss Leung talking to your mother at 10:00AM yesterday?

4. Was / Were the dog eating when you came home?

5. Was / Were Patrick watching football match as the door bell rang?

6. Was / Were they swimming at noon yesterday?

7. Was / Were she playing piano when you saw her?

8. Was / Were they having a barbecue at 2:00PM yesterday?

9. Was / Were grandma making sandwiches when you went out?

10. Was / Were you reading newspaper while he phoned you?

練習二

請參看例子，運用提供的字詞，寫出過去進行式的問句。

例子：Alison / listening to / at 12:00AM last night / was / radio / ?
      Was Alison listening to radio at 12:00AM last night?

1. a car model / you / making / while Simon phoned you / Were / ?

_____

2. Was / playing guitar / at 12:00AM last night / Catherine / ?

_____

3. Were / sleeping / they / as the door bell rang / ?

_____

4. the panda / playing balls / Was / when you saw it / ?

_____

5. Miff and Kitty / Were / when you played piano / singing / ?

_____

6. playing / you / Were / chess / at 11:00AM yesterday / ?

_____

7. grandma / watering / Was / the flowers / while you went home / ?

_____

8. talking / Were / at 11:00PM last night / Uncle John and his friend / ?

_____

9. the cat / Was / running after a mouse / when you saw it / ?

_____

10. washing / was / daddy / dishes / at 8:00PM last night / ?

_____

挑戰站

請將正確答案填在橫線上。

1. _____ Lily _____ (swim) when it _____ (rain)?

2. _____Daisy and Joey _____ (do) homework when daddy_____ (come) home?

3. _____ Andy_____ (have) a barbecue with his classmates at 1:00PM yesterday?

4. _____ you_____ (talk) to Greg as your mother_____(phone) you?

5. _____ Raymond _____ (run) in the playground when you _____(see) him?

6. _____ Julie and Sue _____(listen) to music at 1:00AM last night?

7. _____ Gladys and Peggy_____ (watch) TV when their mummy _____(go) out?

8. _____ Mr. Fairbrother _____(read) story to his child at 9:00PM last night?

9. _____ the cat_____ (sleep) when you _____ (come) home?

10._____ grandpa and grandma _____ (water) the flowers a 8:00AM yesterday?

將來式：
肯定句

Future Tense:
Positive Form

珊珊和家人將會移居美國，她的好朋友小美到機場送行。小美一邊握着珊珊的手，一邊說：「I'll miss you.」（我會想念你。）「I will remember you.」（我會記住你。）小美說的話，屬於哪一種時態呢？

其實，小美說的話屬於將來式（或未來式）時態。**將來式主要用來表達將來的情況或狀態**，即描述在未來的一段時間裡將會發生的事情。

大家看看以下的時間線圖：

| Yesterday | Today | Tomorrow |
| 昨天 | 今天 | 明天 |

Kenny will play football tomorrow.

肯尼明天會踢足球。

「Kenny will play football tomorrow.」是將來式的肯定句形式（The Positive Form），大家留意句子裡用助動詞「will」來表示動詞「play」這個動作是將來才會做的；而句末的「tomorrow」是表示將來的時間字詞。

句式放大鏡

| Kenny | will | play | football | tomorrow. |
| | 助動詞 | 動詞基本形 | | 表示將來的時間的字詞 |

表示將來的字詞

　　一般來說，描述將會發生的事情時，句子通常都會與一些表示「將來的時間」的字詞連用，而且它們通常都會出現在句末。這些字詞包括：in the future（將來）、tomorrow（明天）、soon（不久）、later（稍後/遲些）、next week（下星期）、three days later（三天後）、this coming Saturday（這個星期六）等等。

　　大家要留意，有些句子雖然沒有表示將來的時間的字詞，但它卻表示了將來的情況。我們可從句子中動詞前面出現了助動詞「will」，就知道句子所描述的是將會發生的事情或將來的狀況。

例如：

1. She will be a teacher.
   她將會做老師。

2. Daddy will go to China tomorrow.
   明天爸爸會去中國。

3. I will visit my grandparents next week.
   下星期我會去探望祖父母。

4. They will see a movie this coming Sunday.
   這個星期天他們會去看電影。

> 「shall」和「will」是助動詞，都是含有將來的意思。當句中的主詞是「I」和「We」時，可以選擇用「shall」或「will」，但「will」是比較常用的。
>
> 「shall」和「will」的縮寫是「'll」，如本篇開頭小美對珮珮說：「I'll miss you.」助動詞「shall」和「will」後面接着的動詞必須是基本形，即動詞尾部沒有加「ed」、「s」、「es」等。

文法加油站

練習一

請將正確答案填在橫線上。

1. We _____ (go) to Japan tomorrow.

2. Uncle Mike _____ (leave) Hong Kong next year.

3. I _____ (be) ten years old next year.

4. My sister is three years old. She _____ (be) four years old next month.

5. May _____ (send) this letter to her daddy tomorrow.

6. My uncle _____ (come) from America next Sunday.

7. Kenny _____ (go) to Lamma Island three days later.

8. It _____ (be) sunny this coming Saturday.

9. You _____ (finish) your breakfast soon.

10. He _____ (be) a doctor in the future.

練習二

未來日記：小明在公園裡拾獲一本「Ivan的未來日記」，裡面寫下了日記主人Ivan在2030年3月將會做的事情。

March 2030						
Monday	Tuesday	Wednesday	Thursday	Friday	Saturday	Sunday
		1	2	3	4 go to swim	5
6	7	8	9 play football	10	11	12
13	14	15	16	17	18	19 go to hiking
20	21 play tennis	22	23	24	25	26 go to church
27	28	29	30 play basketball			

請細心觀看上面的日曆，並參看例子，把日記主人將會在哪一天做甚麼事情寫下來。

例子： Ivan will go to swim on 4th March 2030.

1. Ivan will _____

2. Ivan will _____

3. _____

4. _____

5. _____

練習三

參考例子，根據左頁日曆內容，完成下列句子。

例子：The first day of March 2030 will be Wednesday.

1. The fourth day of March 2030 _____ .

2. The ninth day of March 2030 _____ .

3. 19th March, 2030 will be _____ .

4. 21st March, 2030 will be _____ .

5. The last day of March 2030 _____ .

挑戰站

請參看例子，找出下列句子中的錯誤，並將正確的答案寫在右邊的橫線上。

例子：My grandpa will (came) to Hong Kong next month.　　　　come

1. I'll been ten years old. _____

2. I shell send this letter to you tomorrow. _____

3. My uncle shall come from Canada next week. _____

4. We shall goes to swim this coming Sunday. _____

5. He will plays basketball. _____

6. I will visited my friend soon. _____

7. I shall plays football with my classmate tomorrow. _____

8. You shall go to beach with your family. _____

9. The train will leaves at 1:30PM. _____

10. Peggy will been a teacher in the future. _____

chapter 19

將來式：否定句
Future Tense: Negative Form

嘉嘉明天將會參加丁丁的生日派對，她的好朋友思思問她明天會穿甚麼顏色的裙子，嘉嘉回答說：「I will not wear black dress.」（我不會穿黑色裙子。）「I won't wear white dress.」（我不會穿白色裙子。）嘉嘉的話把思思弄糊塗了，到底她要穿甚麼顏色的裙子呢？

其實，嘉嘉的說話屬於將來式（或未來式）時態中的否定句形式。將來式中的否定句形式主要用來**表達在將來的一段時間裡不會發生或不會做的事情。**

大家看看以下的時間線圖：

Last week	This week	Next week
上星期	本星期	下星期

問：What will Tammy not do next week? 答：Tammy will not play tennis next week.
　　譚美下星期不會做甚麼？ 　　譚美下星期不會打網球。

「Tammy will not play tennis next week.」是將來式的否定句形式 (The Negative Form)，大家留意句子中助動詞「will」後接「not」，然後才接動詞基本形「play」，表示有關的動作或事情是將來不會做的；而句末的「next week」是表示將來的時間字詞。

句式放大鏡

Tammy	will	not	play	tennis	next week.
	助動詞	否定	動詞基本形		表示將來的時間的字詞

一般來説，描述將來不會發生的事情時，句中表示將來時態的助動詞「will」和「shall」後面通常都會接「not」，然後才接動詞基本形。

例如：1. Johnny will not be a doctor.
　　　　莊尼不會做醫生。

　　　2. Mr. Chan will not go to Japan tomorrow.
　　　　陳先生明天不會去日本。

　　　3. I shall not visit Uncle Sam next month.
　　　　下個月我不會去探望山姆叔叔。

　　　4. They will not go to swim this coming Saturday.
　　　　這個星期六他們不會去游泳。

> 「shall not」的縮寫是「shan't」；「will not」的縮寫是「won't」，如本篇開頭嘉嘉對思思説：「I won't wear white dress.」
>
> 助動詞否定式「shall not」、「shan't」和「will not」、「won't」後面接着的動詞必須是基本形，即動詞尾部沒有加「ed」、「s」等，如「will not come」、「shall not go」等等。

文法加油站

練習一

請將正確答案填在橫線上。

1. We will stay in Hong Kong. We _____ (go) to America.

2. Dick will be ten years old tomorrow. He _____ (be) eleven years old tomorrow.

3. They will visit Miss Lee this Sunday. They _____ (go) hiking this Sunday.

4. My sister will play tennis next Monday. She _____ (play) badminton next Monday.

5. Kelly will go to sleep at eleven o'clock. She _____ (phone) you at eleven o'clock.

6. Jeff will go to library in the afternoon. He _____ (go) to church in the afternoon.

7. Ken will do homework at four o'clock. He _____ (watch) TV at four o'clock.

8. My Uncle will stay at Lamma Island tomorrow. He _____ (be) at home tomorrow.

9. It will be sunny three days later. It _____ (rain) three days later.

10. We shall play computer game tonight. We _____ (play) football tonight

練習二

請參看例子，把下列肯定句改為否定句。

例子：Ivan will go to Beijing next month.
　　　Ivan will not go to Beijing next month.

1. Miss Chan will come at three o'clock.

_____

2. We shall meet at the MTR station.

_____

3. Tom and Sue will go to the book shop tomorrow.

_____

4. Mum and I will go to the beach this coming Sunday.

    _____ .

5. You will study French in the future.

    _____ .

6. Judy will play tennis with her brother this week.

    _____ .

7. I will have enough money to buy a new pencil box next month.

    _____ .

8. Mummy will tell us the ending of the story tonight.

    _____ .

9. It will be cold three days later.

    _____ .

10. The weather will be good next week.

    _____ .

挑戰站

請參看例子，找出下列句子中的錯誤，並將正確的答案寫在右邊的橫線上。

例子：My grandma (shall) not go to America next year.　　　___will___

1. He'll not be eleven years old next year.　　　_____

2. I shan't came to see you this afternoon.　　　_____

3. My daddy will not worked in China next month.　　　_____

4. We shall not saw a movie tomorrow.　　　_____

5. The weather shall not be good this Sunday.　　　_____

6. You will not watched TV at 11:00PM.　　　_____

7. My classmates and I will no play basketball this Saturday.　　　_____

8. Kitty and Judy shall not go to Shek O with their family
   next week.　　　_____

9. The bus shan't come at 1:15PM.　　　_____

10. Eddie will not played a trick on Joe tonight.　　　_____

chapter 20

將來式：問句

Future Tense: Question Form

　　星期一，弟弟向姐姐借顏色筆，姐姐對弟弟說：「Will you return it to me?」（你會還給我嗎？）弟弟隨口說：「會。」星期三，弟弟向姐姐借字典，姐姐對弟弟說：「Will you return it to me?」（你會還給我嗎？）弟弟仍然隨口說：「會。」星期六，弟弟向姐姐借遊戲機，姐姐有點猶豫，說：「Will you return it to me?」（你會還給我嗎？）弟弟只管盯着遊戲機，隨便點點頭。如果你是姐姐，你會借給他嗎？

　　姐姐說的話屬於將來式（或未來式）時態中的問句形式。將來式中的問句形式主要用來向別人提問**在將來的一段時間裡事情會不會發生**。

大家看看以下的時間線圖：

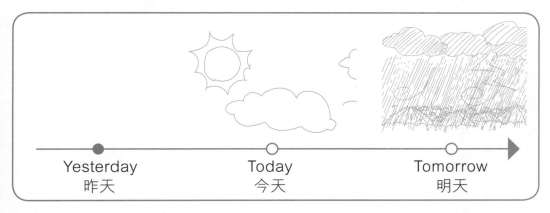

Yesterday	Today	Tomorrow
昨天	今天	明天

問：Will the weather be rainy tomorrow?
　　明天會下雨嗎？

答：Yes, the weather will be rainy tomorrow.
　　是的，明天會下雨。

問：Will the weather be sunny tomorrow?
　　明天會天晴嗎？

答：No, the weather will not be sunny tomorrow.
　　不，明天不會天晴。

　　「Will the weather be rainy tomorrow?」和「Will the weather be sunny tomorrow?」是將來式的問句形式（The Question Form），大家留意問句中的助動詞「will」放在句子的開頭，然後接主詞（或所提問的事物），跟着才接動詞基本形「be」。這種句子用來提問事情在將來**會不會做或會不會發生**。

句式放大鏡

Will	the weather	be	rainy	tomorrow ?
助動詞		動詞基本形		表示將來的時間的字詞

怎樣回答將來式的問句？

回答將來式的問句時，如果答案是肯定的，要用將來式的肯定句來回答，如「Yes, the weather will be rainy tomorrow.」；如果答案是否定的，則要用將來式的否定句來回答，如「No, the weather will not be rainy tomorrow.」。我們再看看下列例子：

1. 問句：Will you be a lawyer in the future?
   你將來會做律師嗎？

   回答－肯定句：Yes, I will be a lawyer in the future.
   是的，我將來會做律師。

   回答－否定句：No, I will not be a lawyer in the future.
   不，我將來不會做律師。

2. 問句：Will daddy go to China next Sunday?
   爸爸下星期天會去中國嗎？

   回答－肯定句：Yes, Daddy will go to China next Sunday.
   是的，爸爸下星期天會去中國。

   回答－否定句：No, Daddy won't go to China next Sunday.
   不，爸爸下星期天不會去中國。

3. 問句：Shall we visit Aunt Amy this coming Saturday?
   這個星期六我們會去探望艾美姨媽嗎？

   回答－肯定句：Yes, we shall visit Aunt Amy this coming Saturday.
   是的，這個星期六我們會去探望艾美姨媽。

   回答－否定句：No, we shall not visit Aunt Amy this coming Saturday.
   不，這個星期六我們不會去探望艾美姨媽。

當句子是問句形式時，助動詞「shall」和「will」必須放在句子的開頭，同時第一個字母必須是大楷（Capital Letter）。

大家要留意上面的例子問句(1)，當問句中的主詞是「you」時，回答時，無論是肯定還是否定，主詞通常都是「I」或「We」。例如：

問：「Will you remember me?」
答：「Yes, I/we will remember you.」

文法加油站

練習一

請參看例子，把將來式中的肯定句改為問句。

例子：Daddy and mummy will go to Japan next week.
      Will daddy and mummy go to Japan next week?

1. They will stay in China this weekend.

_____

2. Dickson and June will join the singing competition.

_____

3. He will visit Aunt Judy next Monday.

_____

4. I will go to Ocean Park this coming Sunday.

_____

5. Anna and Peter will go to library in the afternoon.

_____

練習二

請根據下列各題的回答內容，把將來式的問句寫出來。

1. _____ tomorrow morning?
   Yes, Jeff will go to church tomorrow morning.

2. _____ at eleven o'clock?
   No, Kenney won't watch TV at eleven o'clock.

3. _____ ?
   No, Phoebe will not stay at Lamma Island tonight.

4. _____ ?
   Yes, it will be sunny two days later.

5. _____ ?
   Yes, I will play football with friends tomorrow.

6. _____ ?
   No, Sean won't have a computer in his new bedroom.

7. _____ ?
   Yes, Uncle Ivan will work in America.

8. _____ ?

No, I won't join the piano competition.

9. _____ ?

Yes, we will buy her a cake for her birthday.

10. _____ ?

No, the train will not come at 2:30PM.

挑戰站

請細心閱讀下面的文章，然後回答問題。

It will be public holiday tomorrow. Jacky will go out with his family. They will go to Lamma Island in the morning. They will have seafood for lunch. They will take photos there. They will leave Lamma Island at 6:00PM and will go to Tsim Sha Tsui for dinner. They will go home at 9:00PM.

1. Will it be public holiday tomorrow?

_____

2. Will Jacky go to Shek O with his family?

_____

3. Will they have seafood for lunch?

_____

4. Will they leave Lamma Island at 9:00PM?

_____

5. Will they have lunch at Kowloon Bay?

_____

chapter 21

將來式：
be going to

More about Future Tense: be going to

丁丁和家欣是鄰居，丁丁叫家欣出來玩，家欣說：「I am going to have dinner.」，丁丁覺得奇怪，家欣明明在跟自己談話，為甚麼說在吃晚飯呢？

　　家欣所說的話沒有錯，是丁丁誤會了。「I am going to have dinner.」句中的「be going to」雖然屬於現在進行式的句子，但是它所指的時態卻是將來式的。「be going to」主要用來表達**將來肯定會發生的動作、情況或狀態。**

大家看看以下的時間線圖：

Yesterday	Today	Tomorrow
昨天	今天	明天

Tom is going to buy a computer tomorrow.
明天湯姆會買一台電腦。

句式放大鏡

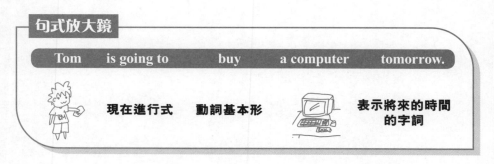

Tom	is going to	buy	a computer	tomorrow.
	現在進行式	動詞基本形		表示將來的時間的字詞

「Tom is going to buy a computer tomorrow.」是現在進行式的句子，可以用來表達將來會發生的動作和情況。當句子出現「be going to」，而句尾同時出現表示將來的時間的字詞時，我們就可以肯定這個動作或情況是將來會做或發生的。

同樣，在表達將來會發生的事情時，句子通常都會與一些表示「將來的時間」的字詞連用，而且它們通常都會出現在句末。這些字詞包括：in the future（將來）、tomorrow（明天）、soon（不久）、later（稍後/遲些）、next week（下星期）等等。
例如：

She is going to be a doctor next year .
明年她會做醫生。

I am going to have dinner with my friend soon .
稍後我會和朋友吃晚飯。

The children are going to watch the show with Miss Lee tonight .
今晚孩子們會和李老師去看表演。

文法加油站

請用 be going to 完成下列句子。

1. Sam and Alison _____ (go) to Italy tomorrow.

2. Mandy _____ (talk) about a very serious matter.

3. I _____ (be) a lawyer next year.

4. My grandpa _____ (be) seventy years old next month.

5. They _____ (see) this movie tonight.

6. Amanda and Johnny_____ (have) dinner soon.

7. He _____ (study) at four o'clock.

8. It _____ (be) rainy tomorrow.

9. We _____ (make) a chocolate cake tonight.

10. The children _____ (swim) at two o'clock.

練習二

請參看例子，運用提供的字詞，寫出含有 be going to 的句子。

例子：Abbie / cook / soon / is going to / .
　　　Abbie is going to cook soon.

1. a model / Daddy and Tom / make / are going to / tonight / .

_____

2. is going to / play / in the afternoon / Simon / football / .

_____

3. are going to / see / tonight / they / the football match / .

_____

4. it / tomorrow / cloudy / is going to / be / .

_____

5. Maggie and Kitty / have / are going to / dinner / tonight / .

_____

小學生學 *Grammar* ── 句子文法

95

6. play / Kerry and you / are going to / chess / at four o'clock / .

_____

7. She / go / is going to / this Sunday / hiking / .

_____

8. read / is going to / at 11:00PM tonight / Uncle David / .

_____

9. I / visit / am going to / my grandparents / next weekend / .

_____

10. play / are going to / We / soon / computer game / .

_____

挑戰站

請參看例子，找出下列句子中的錯誤，並將正確的答案寫在右邊的橫線上。

例子：

1. Daddy is going ∧ go China tomorrow.   to

2. They (is) going to play football soon.   are

3. She is going to (saw) her grandma next week.   see

1. I are going to be twelve years old next week. _____

2. They are going to swimming in the afternoon. _____

3. Kathy is going visit Peter next week. _____

4. We is going to get married next month. _____

5. The children am going to make a car model tonight. _____

6. Tom and Sam are going see the show tomorrow. _____

7. I am going to plays football with Frankie at four o'clock. _____

8. You am going to have dinner with your family tonight. _____

9. The train is going to leaves at 4:00PM tomorrow. _____

10. Tony and Lily are going to left Hong Kong next Sunday. _____

綜合挑戰站

練習一

請利用提供的字詞，寫出正確的陳述句。（提示：注意動詞的時態）

例子：Peter / saw

Peter saw a movie yesterday.

1. Nancy / visit

_____

2. They / like

_____

3. We / swam

_____

4. Kitty and Sandy / cook

_____

5. Raymond / made

_____

_____

練習二

請利用提供的字詞，寫出正確的問句。（提示：注意動詞的時態）

例子：What / see

What does Peter see?

. Can / come

_____

. Will / stay

_____

. Did / swim

_____

. Who / Kitty and Sandy

_____

. Do / like

_____

練習三

請利用提供的字詞，寫出正確的感嘆句。（提示：注意動詞的時態）

例子：What / beautiful

What a beautiful baby!

1. Great

_____

2. Long / How

_____

3. Lovely / A

_____

4. done / Well

_____

5. Beautiful

_____

練習四

請細閱下文，並填上正確的答案。

Yesterday Uncle Ray and Aunt Amy 1. _____ (come) to Hong Kong. Daddy and

mommy 2. _____ (show) them around Hong Kong. We 3. _____ (have) tea

in a Chinese restaurant in the morning. We 4. _____ (go) to shopping in

Mongkok and Causeway Bay in the afternoon. We 5. _____ (go) to the Peak a

eight o'clock. Uncle Ray and Aunt Amy 6. _____ (have) a nice day.

Today we 7. _____ (go) to Lamma Island with Uncle Ray and Aunt Amy. W

8. _____ (go) to Tai O first. It 9. _____ (be) a wonderful village. Th

houses in Tai O 10. _____ (be) very interesting. We 11. _____ (have) seafoo in lunch time. Uncle Ray 12. _____ (take) some photos there. Aunt Amy

13. _____ (like) the nature environment so much. They 14. _____ (feel)

very happy today.

     Uncle Ray and Aunt Amy 15. _____ (leave) for Macao tomorrow. They

16. _____ (travel) China then. Daddy, mommy and I 17. _____

(send) Uncle Ray and Aunt Amy to the pier. I 18. _____ (present) Aunt Amy a

small gift.

練習五

請圈出句中的名詞和動詞。

1. Janice is a girl.

2. Tommy and David love playing football.

3. The man and the woman are my parents.

4. Miss Fong is a nice teacher.

5. Sam passed the salt to me.

6. Daddy doesn't like smoking.

7. Alice likes drinking coffee.

8. The cat is cute!

9. Hong Kong is a wonderful place.

10. Donna and Jack were in the same class last year.

綜合挑戰站

練習六

請圈出句中的副詞和形容詞。

1. How beautiful!

2. The dog is big.

3. The baby is cute.

4. He always goes to bed at ten o'clock.

5. I will study in America next year.

6. Mr. Lee came here a few minutes ago.

7. Nancy's dress is as beautiful as yours.

8. Peter is taller than David.

9. He runs fast.

10. He speaks carefully.

全書練習答案

Chapter 1 文法加油站

練習一

1. ✓ 2. ✓ 3. ✓ 4. ✓ 5. ✓ 6. ✗ 7. ✗ 8. ✓ 9. ✓ 10. ✗

練習二

1. S 2. S 3. E 4. Q 5. S 6. S 7. E 8. Q 9. S 10. E

挑戰站

1. Bobby is my dog.
2. Carrie and Janice were in the same class last year.
3. Have he come?
4. A handsome boy!
5. How beautiful!
6. I go hiking with Sidney.
7. Have you read this book?
8. Daddy watched football match at ten o'clock.
9. She cried.
10. We had a barbecue in Shek O last week.

Chapter 2 文法加油站

練習一

1. ✗ 2. ✓ 3. ✓ 4. ✓ 5. ✗ 6. ✗ 7. ✓ 8. ✓ 9. ✓ 10. ✓

練習二

1. Let	2. Don't	3. Be	4. Don't	5. Stop
6. Be / Tell	7. Wake	8. Let's	9. Write	10. Don't

挑戰站

1. [Kept] Keep	2. [Doesn't] Don't
3. [is] be	4. [Been] Be
5. [Looking] Look	6. [Let] Let's
7. [talked] talk	8. [Woke] Wake
9. [Listening] Listen	10. [running] run

Chapter 3 文法加油站

練習一

1. [are] ✓	2. [goes] ✓	3. ✗	4. [like] ✓	5. ✗
6. [are] ✓	7. [is] ✓	8. [wants] ✓	9. [is] ✓	10. [leaves] ✓

練習二

1. is	2. has	3. am	4. like	5. swims
6. are	7. wakes	8. is	9. watch	10. want

挑戰站

1. [were] is	2. [was] is
3. [come] comes	4. [goes] go
5. [playes] plays	6. [visited] visit

7. [likes] like   8. [went] go
9. [leave] leaves   10. [be] is

Chapter 4 文法加油站
練習一
1. ✗   2. [does not go] ✓
3. [am not] ✓   4. [do not like] ✓
5. [do not have] ✓   6. [is not] ✓
7. ✗   8. [does not want] ✓
9. ✗   10. [does not arrive] ✓

練習二
1. is not   2. does not have   3. is not   4. does not sleep   5. does not want
6. are not   7. does not go   8. is not   9. am not   10. do not watch

挑戰站
1. Chris does not like coffee.
2. I am not a teacher.
3. Mr. Smith does not come from Australia.
4. We do not go to the beach this weekend.
5. I do not play tennis with Sue.
6. Miranda and Kitty do not visit Lily this Saturday.
7. Greg and Amy do not like singing.
8. Mummy does not go to supermarket.
9. The dog is not small.
10. Charlie is not my classmate.

Chapter 5 文法加油站
練習一
1. Do   2. Do   3. Do   4. Does   5. Does
6. Does   7. Do   8. Does   9. Do

練習二
1. Am   2. Is   3. Am   4. Is   5. Are
6. Are   7. Is   8. Is   9. Is   10. Is

挑戰站
1. [Am]   Is
2. [Do]   Does
3. [has]   have
4. [goes] go
5. [Are]   Is
6. [Does] Do
7. [Am]   Are
8. [Is]   Are
9. [leaves] leave
10. [Are] Is

Chapter 6 文法加油站
練習一
1. Kenny and Mandy are running away.
2. Mummy is cooking in the kitchen.

3. I am taking the bus.

4. You are playing football with your classmates.

5. We are having barbecue.

6. They are watching TV.

7. The bus is coming.

8. She is eating some cookies.

9. A dog is running after a cat.

10. Adrian is putting the book on the table.

練習二

1. swimming	2. watching	3. getting	4. sitting	5. running
6. driving	7. having	8. teaching	9. writing	10. reading
11. singing	12. cooking	13. flying	14. walking	15. cutting

挑戰站

1. [geting]   getting

2. [makeing]   making

3. [am]   is

4. [is]   are

5. [am]   is

6. [driveing]   driving

7. [cookking]   cooking

8. [puting]   putting

9. [comeing]   coming

10. [singging]   singing

Chapter 7　文法加油站

練習一

1. Jessica and May are not cooking in the kitchen.

2. Grandma is not sitting on the sofa.

3. I am not watching TV.

4. You are not playing table tennis with Tammy.

5. We are not making car model.

6. They are not washing dishes.

7. The dog is not eating fish.

8. Betty is not making sandwiches.

9. Ben and Eric are not singing in the music room.

10. Janice is not putting the bag on the table.

練習二

1. ✓　2. ✗　3. ✓　4. ✓　5. ✓　6. ✓　7. ✗　8. ✓　9. ✗　10. ✓

挑戰站

1. [geting]   getting

2. [driveing]   driving

3. [am]   is

4. [am no]   are not

5. [no playying]   not playing

6. [drinkking]   drinking

7. [no cookking]   not cooking

8. [is no]   are not

9. [no]   not

10. [am no]   is not

Chapter 8　文法加油站

練習一

1. Am　2. Are　3. Is　4. Is　5. Are　6. Are　7. Is　8. Are　9. Is　10. Are

練習二

1. Am I drawing a car?

2. Is Winnie talking to her mother?

3. Are Tammy and Peggy washing dishes?

4. Is the panda eating bamboo?

5. Are Kitty and Pat singing in the music room?

6. Are you playing chess with Sam?

7. Is grandpa watering flowers in the garden?

8. Am I making day dream?

9. Is the weather getting worse?

10. Is mummy watching TV in the sitting room?

挑戰站

1. [Am]　Is		2. [Are]　Is	
3. [haveing]　having		4. [Am]　Are	
5. [singging]　singing		6. [!]　?	
7. [watched]　watching		8. [readding]　reading	
9. [comeing]　coming		10. [.]　?	

Chapter 9　文法加油站

練習一

1. made	2. sold	3. taken	4. gone	5. done
6. had	7. been	8. sung	9. talked	10. put
11. cut	12. ridden	13. learned	14. left	15. got/gotten

練習二

1. [have been] ✓　　　　　2. ✗

3. [have gone] ✓　　　　　4. [have] [made] ✓

5. [have] [seen] ✓　　　　6. ✗

7. [has been] ✓　　　　　8. ✗

9. [have] [done] ✓　　　　10. [has] [left] ✓

挑戰站

1. has been　　2. has played

3. have lived　　4. has learned

5. have come　　6. have been

7. have put　　8. has managed

9. have worked　　10. has mended

Chapter 10　文法加油站

練習一

1. ✗　2. ✓　3. ✓　4. ✗　5. ✓　6. ✗　7. ✓　8. ✗　9. ✓　10. ✓

練習二

1. been	2. played	3. studied	4. made	5. watered
6. finished	7. rung	8. received	9. left	10. bought

挑戰站

1. [no finishhed]　not finished

2. [has]　have

3. [work]　worked

4. [has no buy]　have not bought

5. [have]　has

6. [has]　have

7. [make]　made

8. [no sleep]　not slept

9. [arrive]　arrived

10. [have no]　has not

Chapter 11　文法加油站

練習一

| 1. Has | 2. Has | 3. Have | 4. Has | 5. Have |
| 6. Has | 7. Have | 8. Has | 9. Have | 10. Has |

練習二

1. Have they finished the dinner yet?
2. Have Jessica and Vincent left yet?
3. Has she ever seen this movie?
4. Have they made the model yet?
5. Have Ken and Amy lived in Kowloon Bay?
6. Have Francis and you ever been in the same class?
7. Have you played with my dog?
8. Has mummy ever made a pizza?
9. Has Hong Kong been a fishing village?
10. Have the children done their homework yet?

挑戰站

1. [be]　been
2. [go]　gone
3. [find]　found
4. [clean]　cleaned
5. [dance]　danced
6. [saw]　seen
7. [Has]　Have
8. [Has]　Have
9. [finish]　finished
10. [Have]　Has

Chapter 12　文法加油站

練習一

| 1. [were] ✓ | 2. ✗ | 3. ✗ | 4. [played] ✓ | 5. [had] ✓ |
| 6. ✗ | 7. [was] ✓ | 8. ✗ | 9. [was] ✓ | 10. [made] ✓ |

練習二

| 1. was | 2. had | 3. was | 4. won | 5. put |
| 6. saw | 7. helped | 8. was | 9. dressed | 10. went |

挑戰站

1. Amy helped grandpa watering flowers last Tuesday.
2. Amy played piano at home last Tuesday.
3. Amy helped mummy making a chocolate cake last Wednesday.
4. Amy had a story time with mummy before going to bed last Wednesday.
5. Amy had a walk with grandpa after dinner last Thursday.
6. Amy visited Aunt Sharon at 6:00PM last Friday.
7. Amy played computer game with her cousin at Aunt Sharon's home last Friday.
8. Amy went to Hong Kong Disneyland with daddy and mummy last Saturday.
9. Amy cleaned her room last Sunday.
10. Amy had dinner with her family at Sun Sun Restaurant last Sunday.

Chapter 13　文法加油站

練習一

1. ✗   2. [were not] ✓
3. [was not] ✓   4. [did not go] ✓
5. [did not have] ✓   6. ✗
7. [was not] ✓   8. [did not see] ✓
9. [was not] ✓   10. [did not eat] ✓

練習二

1. were not	2. did not dress	3. was not	4. did not sleep	5. did not make
6. did not see	7. did not go	8. was not	9. was not	10. did not watch

挑戰站

1. Jacky and Stella were not in Hong Kong last week.
2. Miss Lee was not a teacher in the past.
3. I did not watch the football match last night.
4. You did not attend the swimming class last Monday.
5. We did not make a model a few days ago.
6. The children did not play chess a few hours ago.
7. The cat did not go home yesterday.
8. Tim did not see the accident last night.
9. Ben and Eric were not in the same class last year.
10. Francis did not put the glasses on the table a few hours ago.

Chapter 14　文法加油站

練習一

1. Was	2. Did	3. Was	4. Did	5. Did
6. Did	7. Did	8. Were	9. Did	10. Was

練習二

1. Was he late yesterday?
2. Did Judy go home at eleven o' clock?
3. Did they see a movie last week?
4. Was grandma a beautiful lady when she was young?
5. Did Ken live in Tai Po a few years ago?
6. Were Tammy and you in the same class last year?
7. Did Susan draw a panda a few hours ago?
8. Did mummy make an apple pie last night?
9. Was the weather cloudy last Sunday?
10. Did the children fight yesterday?

挑戰站

1. [Were]　Was
2. [Was]　Did
3. [made]　make
4. [Did]　Was
5. [Did]　Was
6. [Were]　Was
7. [Did]　Were
8. [Was]　Did
9. [Were]　Did
10. [Was]　Did

Chapter 15 文法加油站

練習一

1. ✓ 2. ✓ 3. ✗ 4. ✗ 5. ✗ 6. ✓ 7. ✗ 8. ✓ 9. ✓ 10. ✗

練習二

1. [were]   was   2. [watchhing]   watching
3. [ring]   rang   4. [readding]   reading
5. [was haveing]   were having   6. [was]   were
7. [meet]   met   8. [was]   were
9. [see]   saw   10. [was talkking]   were talking

挑戰站

1. Peter was sleeping when the theft entered his house.
2. Paul and Jimmy were making model while the door bell rang.
3. Mrs. Cheung was writing as Mr. Cheung came home.
4. We were playing computer game while Sally came.
5. Tom was drawing when his grandma went out.
6. I was walking when the accident happened.
7. Tammy and Elsa were swimming when it rained.
8. You were sleeping when Aunt Amy visited.
9. I was eating while the phone rang.
10. Daddy was having breakfast as I woke up.

Chapter 16 文法加油站

練習一

1. Sam and May were not watching TV at 9:00PM last night.
2. Uncle Ray was not reading in the afternoon yesterday.
3. I was not doing homework while daddy came home.
4. Amy and you were not playing tennis when it rained.
5. Simon was not making car model when I saw him.
6. Mummy was not washing dishes at 8:00PM last night.
7. The dog was not sleeping when I came home.
8. Benny and Kitty were not making sandwiches at noon yesterday.
9. Tammy and Eric were not singing at 12:00PM last night.
10. Brenda was not shopping when the accident happened.

練習二

1. ✗ 2. ✓ 3. ✓ 4. ✓ 5. ✗ 6. ✓ 7. ✗ 8. ✓ 9. ✗ 10. ✓

挑戰站

1. [is]   was

2. [no driveing]   not driving

3. [were]   was

4. [was no]   were not

5. [was no playying]   were not playing

6. [were]   was

7. [no]   not

8. [were no]   was not

9. [no runing]   not running

10. [sleeping]   sleeping

Chapter 17　文法加油站

練習一

1. Was	2. Were	3. Was	4. Was	5. Was
6. Were	7. Was	8. Were	9. Was	10. Were

練習二

1. Were you making a car model while Simon phoned you?
2. Was Catherine playing guitar at 12:00AM last night?
3. Were they sleeping as the door bell rang?
4. Was the panda playing balls when you saw it?
5. Were Miff and Kitty singing when you played piano?
6. Were you playing chess at 11:00AM yesterday?
7. Was grandma watering the flowers while you went home?
8. Were Uncle John and his friend talking at 11:00PM last night?
9. Was the cat running after a mouse when you saw it?
10. Was daddy washing dishes at 8:00PM last night?

挑戰站

1. Was, swimming, rained
2. Were, doing, came
3. Was, having
4. Were, talking, phoned
5. Was, running, saw
6. Were, listening
7. Were, watching, went
8. Was, reading
9. Was, sleeping, came
10. Were, watering

Chapter 18　文法加油站

練習一

1. will/shall go	2. will leave	3. will/shall be	4. will be	5. will send
6. will come	7. will go	8. will be	9. will finish	10. will be

練習二

1. Ivan will play football on 9th March 2030.
2. Ivan will go to hiking on 19th March 2030.
3. Ivan will play tennis on 21st March 2030.
4. Ivan will go to church on 26th March 2030.
5. Ivan will play basketball on 30th March 2030.

練習三

1. The fourth day of March 2030 will be Saturday.
2. The ninth day of March 2030 will be Thursday.
3. 19th March, 2030 will be Sunday.
4. 21st March, 2030 will be Tuesday.
5. The last day of March 2030 will be Thursday.

挑戰站

1. [been]　be	2. [shell]　shall	3. [shall]　will
4. [goes]　go	5. [plays]　play	6. [visited]　visit
7. [plays]　play	8. [shall]　will	9. [leaves]　leave
10.[been]　be		

Chapter 19　文法加油站

練習一

1. will/shall not go
2. will not be
3. will not go
4. will not play
5. will not phone
6. will not go
7. will not watch
8. will not be
9. will not rain
10. shall not play

練習二

1. Miss Chan will not come at three o'clock.
2. We shall not meet at the MTR station.
3. Tom and Sue will not go to the book shop tomorrow.
4. Mum and I will not go to the beach this coming Sunday.
5. You will not study French in the future.
6. Judy will not play tennis with her brother this week.
7. I will not have enough money to buy a new pencil box next month.
8. Mummy will not tell us the ending of the story tonight.
9. It will not be cold three days later.
10. The weather will not be good next week.

挑戰站

1. ['ll not]　won't
2. [came]　come
3. [worked]　work
4. [saw]　see
5. [shall]　will
6. [watched]　watch
7. [no]　not
8. [shall]　will
9. [shan't]　won't
10. [played]　play

Chapter 20　文法加油站

練習一

1. Will they stay in China this weekend?
2. Will Dickson and June join the singing competition?
3. Will he visit Aunt Judy next Monday?
4. Will you go to Ocean Park this coming Sunday?
5. Will Anna and Peter go to library in the afternoon?

練習二

1. Will Jeff go to church tomorrow morning?
2. Will Kenney watch TV at eleven o'clock?
3. Will Phoebe stay at Lamma Island tonight?
4. Will it be sunny two days later?
5. Will you play football with friends tomorrow?
6. Will Sean have a computer in his new bedroom?
7. Will Uncle Ivan work in America?
8. Will you join the piano competition?
9. Will you buy her a cake for her birthday?
10. Will the train come at 2:30PM?

挑戰站

1. Yes, it will be public holiday tomorrow.
2. No, Jacky will not / won't go to Shek O with his family.
3. Yes, they will have seafood for lunch.
4. No, they will not / won't leave Lamma Island at 9:00PM.
5. No, they will not / won't have lunch at Kowloon Bay.

Chapter 21　文法加油站

練習一

1. are going to go
2. is going to talk
3. am going to be
4. is going to be
5. are going to see
6. are going to have
7. is going to study
8. is going to be
9. are going to make
10. are going to swim

練習二

1. Daddy and Tom are going to make a model tonight.
2. Simon is going to play football in the afternoon.
3. They are going to see the football match tonight.
4. It is going to be cloudy tomorrow.
5. Maggie and Kitty are going to have dinner tonight.
6. Kerry and you are going to play chess at four o'clock.
7. She is going to go hiking this Sunday.
8. Uncle David is going to read at 11:00PM tonight.
9. I am going to visit my grandparents next weekend.
10. We are going to play computer game soon.

挑戰站

1. [are]　am
2. [swimming]　swim
3. going ∧ to visit
4. [is]　are
5. [am]　are
6. going ∧ to see
7. [plays]　play
8. [am]　are
9. [leaves]　leave
10. [left]　leave

Chapter 22　綜合挑戰站

練習一

1. Nancy visits her grandpa today.
2. They like swimming.
3. We swam in the swimming pool yesterday.
4. Kitty and Sandy cook themselves.
5. Raymond made a car model last night.

練習二
1. Can Peter come?
2. Will you stay here?
3. Did you swim last week?
4. Who are Kitty and Sandy?
5. Do you like singing?

練習三

1. Great!   2. How Long!   3. A Lovely doll!   4. Well done!   5. Beautiful!

練習四

1. came   2. showed

3. had   4. went

5. went   6. had

7. go   8. go

9. is   10. are

11. have   12. takes

13. likes   14. feel

15. will leave / are going to leave

16. will travel / are going to travel

17. will send / are going to send

18. will present / am going to present

練習五

1. [Janice] [is] a [girl].
2. [Tommy and David] [love] playing [football].
3. The [man] and the [woman] [are] my [parents].
4. [Miss Fong] [is] a nice [teacher].
5. [Sam] [passed] the [salt] to me.
6. [Daddy] doesn't [like] smoking.
7. [Alice] [likes] drinking [coffee].
8. The [cat] [is] cute!
9. [Hong Kong] [is] a wonderful [place].
10. [Donna and Jack] [were] in the same [class] last year.

練習六

1. How [beautiful]!
2. The dog is [big].
3. The baby is [cute].
4. He [always] goes to bed at ten o'clock.
5. I will study in America [next year].
6. Mr. Lee came [here] a few minutes [ago].
7. Nancy's dress is as [beautiful] as yours.
8. Peter is [taller] than David.
9. He runs [fast].
10. He speaks [carefully].

《小學生學 Grammar —— 圖解教程和練習 (句子文法)》

編著：李雪熒
責任編輯：蘇飛、高家華
封面及版面設計：麥碧心
插圖：王美琪

出版：跨版生活圖書出版
地址：荃灣沙咀道 11-19 號達貿中心 211 室
電話：3153 5574　　　　傳真：3162 7223
專頁：http://www.facebook.com/crossborderbook
網站：http://www.crossborderbook.net
電郵：crossborderbook@yahoo.com.hk

發行：泛華發行代理有限公司
地址：香港新界將軍澳工業邨駿昌街 7 號星島新聞集團大廈
電話：2798 2220　　　　傳真：2796 5471
網頁：http://www.gccd.com.hk
電郵：gccd@singtaonewscorp.com

台灣總經銷：永盈出版行銷有限公司
地址：231 新北市新店區中正路 499 號 4 樓
電話：(02)2218 0701　　　　傳真：(02)2218 0704

印刷：鴻基印刷有限公司

出版日期：2021 年 3 月第三版
定價：HK$88　NT$350
ISBN：978-988-78897-0-0

出版社法律顧問：勞潔儀律師行